2004 POETRY C

ONCE UPON A RHYME

IMAGINATION FOR
A NEW GENERATION

Scotland Vol II
Edited by Steve Twelvetree

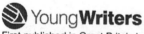 Young**Writers**

First published in Great Britain in 2004 by:
Young Writers
Remus House
Coltsfoot Drive
Peterborough
PE2 9JX
Telephone: 01733 890066
Website: www.youngwriters.co.uk

SB ISBN 1 84460 616 3

Foreword

Young Writers was established in 1991 and has been passionately devoted to the promotion of reading and writing in children and young adults ever since. The quest continues today. Young Writers remains as committed to engendering the fostering of burgeoning poetic and literary talent as ever.

This year's Young Writers competition has proven as vibrant and dynamic as ever and we are delighted to present a showcase of the best poetry from across the UK. Each poem has been carefully selected from a wealth of *Once Upon A Rhyme* entries before ultimately being published in this, our twelfth primary school poetry series.

Once again, we have been supremely impressed by the overall high quality of the entries we have received. The imagination, energy and creativity which has gone into each young writer's entry made choosing the best poems a challenging and often difficult but ultimately hugely rewarding task - the general high standard of the work submitted amply vindicating this opportunity to bring their poetry to a larger appreciative audience.

We sincerely hope you are pleased with our final selection and that you will enjoy *Once Upon A Rhyme Scotland Vol II* for many years to come.

Contents

Daryl Scott (11) 17
Dean Morison (10) 17
Henna Khan (9) 18
Kennedy Duncan (8) 18
Jade Fraser (8) 19
Adele West (8) 19
Jordan Paterson (9) 19
Jennifer Bruce (8) 20
Erin Sutherland (8) 20
Vanessa Wood (9) 21
Shaun Priest (8) 21
Bethan Coady (8) 22
Jack Duncan (8) 22
Chloe Low (9) 23
Scott Wilson (8) 23
Laura Mathers (11) 24
Luke Mackenzie (8) 24
Kelsie Haggerty (7) 25
Hilary McArthur (8) 25

Bervie Primary School, Montrose

Shanna Yeats (11) 26
Sean Tait (10) 26
Stuart Crockett (11) 26
Callum Ogilvie (11) 27
Scott McKenzie (12) 27
Daniel Taylor (12) 27
Ashley Simpson (11) 28
Daniel Robb (11) 28
Peter Harden (11) 29
Rebecca Metcalfe (12) 29
Jacqui Kerr (11) 30
Amy Jamieson (10) 30
Cameron Woodger (10) 30
Lyndsay Jarvie (11) 31
Gemma Lamb (10) 31
Becky MacQueen (10) 31
Andrew Benton (11) 32

Clerkhill School, Peterhead

Kyle Ritchie (8)	32
Sean Henderson (9)	32
Rosanne Borthwick (8)	33
Gillian Tait (9)	33
Joshua Ward (8)	33
Rachel Fakley (8)	34
Jade Mair (8)	34
Eve Davidson (8)	35
Catherine Ritchie (10)	35
Jennifer Rhynd (10)	36
Laura Chalk (9)	36

Collydean Primary School, Glenrothes

Lauren Mitchell (10)	36
Alex Marjoram (11)	37
Bradley Murray (10)	37
Stephanie Arnott (10)	38
Emma Robertson (10)	38
Kimberley Webster (8)	39
Stuart Callison (10)	39
Ashley Roy (11)	40
Michelle Proudfoot (10)	40
Douglas Gold (12)	41
Megan Rutherford (10)	41
Kevin Kerr (10)	42
Danni McGough (10)	42
Josh Mills (10)	43
Laura Barrett (11)	43
Rachael Smith (11)	44
Sarah Campbell (8)	44
Claire Pollock (10)	45
Jessica Smith (10)	45
Nick Mitchell (11)	46
Marissa Kennedy (10)	46
Kirsty Cheape (11)	47
Luke Beimers (12)	47
Stacey Clark (10)	47
Rebecca Robb (9)	48
Jodie McKellar (10)	48
Lisa Proudfoot (12)	49

Phoebe Brown (10)	49
Gemma Grieve (9)	50
Lindsey McKerrell (8)	50
Warren Gibson (10)	51
Carrie Deavin (11)	51
Aaron Campbell (9)	52
Rebekah Brown (11)	52
Aimee Husband (9)	53
Helen Bashforth (11)	53
Louise Leslie (10)	54
Kelsey Sloane-Pirrie (10)	55
Emily Reid (10)	56
Sam Randall (9)	56
Kirsten Clunie (9)	57
Rhianne Pye (11)	57
Katy Horsburgh (10)	58
Johnny Campbell (11)	58
Carolanne Campbell (9)	59
Rebecca Edmonston (10)	59
Trudy Hamilton (9)	60
Rebecca Forbes (11)	61
Danielle Woodford (12)	61
Jack Robb (8)	62
Sean McGrath (11)	62
Graeme Marnie (11)	63
Andrew Whiteley (11)	63
Bruce Campbell (10)	64
Charlie Campbell (11)	64
Sara Ward (11)	64
John Douglas (12)	65
Ryan McNeill (10)	65
Kyle Farmer (11)	66
Kayleigh McGough (12)	66
Michelle Laing (10)	66
Logan Watt (10)	67
Hayley Burnett (8)	67
Samantha Morgan (11)	68
Lucy Metcalfe (10)	68
Farhan Ahmed (10)	68
Jemma Black (10)	69
Kyle Maguire (10)	69
Danielle McSherry-Schee (12)	70

Christopher Mackay (11)	70
Shannon Blackwood (10)	70
Ross Jeffrey (10)	71
Stephanie Hopkins (11)	71
April Lavelle (11)	71
Vanessa Gordon (11)	72
Natasha Clugston (10)	72
Lorraine Brown (11)	73
Shannon Smith (11)	73
Amy McAteer (11)	74
Grant Fenton (11)	74
Stasi Brogan (10)	75
Scott Menzies (11)	75
Sean Ramage (8)	75
Amy Hall (8)	76
Curtis Edwards (8)	76
Gary Dillon (8)	76
Chelsea Gourlay (8)	77
Daniel Whiteley (8)	77
Amy Walker (8)	77
John Chapman (11)	78
Aimee Thomson (11)	78
Jake Brown (8)	78
Lindsey Gassner (11)	79
Emma Jex (11)	79
Jasmine Stenhouse (10)	80
Scott McKeen (9)	80
Peter Woodbridge (9)	81
Rachel Scott (10)	81
Shannon Batchelor (9)	82
Rachel Barnet (9)	82
John McArthur (9)	83
Barry Farmer (11)	83
Rebecca Wilson (10)	84
Gina Bishop (10)	84
Keith Rodger (11)	85
George Morrison (11)	85
Kyle Harrower (10)	86
Stefanie Heron (8)	86
Sean Perrie (9)	87
Hayley McKenna (8)	87
Sean Farrell (10)	88

Morgan Swan (10)	89
Kenneth Morris (8)	89
Shannon Blaney (10)	90
Michael Currie (8)	90
Steven Smith (9)	91
Aletia Robertson (8)	91
Nicola Forsyth (9)	92
Nicola Gallacher (10)	93
Hannah Blackwood (9)	94
Callum Penman (8)	94
Phillipa Drummond (10)	95
Kane Easson (10)	95
Corey Carnegie (9)	96
Hannah Pollock (8)	96
Craig Ross (10)	96
Scott Blackwood (11)	97
Chelsie Courts (10)	97

Cranshaws Primary School, Duns
Corin Arkieson (7)	97

Crossgates Primary School, Cowdenbeath
Jodie Nardone (10)	98
Alyssa Lax (9)	99
Ross Shepherd (9)	99
Sarah Turner (9)	100
Jake Simpson (9)	100
Emma Park (9)	101
Chloe Meiklem (9)	101
Imogen Brindle (10)	102
Lindsay McGouldrick (9)	102
Ben Polhill (9)	103
Carly Miller (9)	103
Claire Cuthill (9)	104
Sam Penman (9)	104
Kara Westwood (9)	105
Steven Murphy (9)	105

Cullen Primary School, Buckie
Shaun Mitchell (11)	106
Liam Donn (11)	106

Christopher Gray (11)   107
Suzanne Grant (12)   107
Chloe McCluskey (11)   108
Morven Robb (12)   108
Amber Cox (11)   109
Ben Addison (12)   109
Grace Joyce (11)   110
Lydia Francis (11)   111
Sasha Reid (11)   111
Chloe McGregor (12)   112
David Allan (12)   113
Melissa Mair (11)   113
James Morrison (11)   114
Judith Mair (11)   114
Emma Hay (12)   115

Eccles/Leitholm Primary School, Kelso
Katrina Hay (11)   115
Jade Hebdon (11)   116
Charlie Davis (10)   116
Hope Brown (11)   117

Kenmore Primary School, Kenmore by Aberfeldy
Shekira James (8)   117
Chloe Bennett (9)   118
Rosie Harrison Flower (9)   118
Munro Fraser (8)   119
Bradley Baird (10)   119
Rosie Jo Thomas (8)   120
Robbie Olivier (9)   120

Muck Primary School, Mallaig
Isobel Murray John (7)   120
Amy McFadzean (9)   121
Jamie MacEwen (8)   121

Newhall Primary School, Dingwall
Eilidh MacKenzie (11)   122
Victoria Hammond (10)   122
Ryan Gault (11)   123

New Pitsligo & St Johns Primary School, Fraserburgh

Parkhill Primary School, Leven

Pittenweem Primary School, Pittenweem

St Blanes Primary School, Glasgow

Jacklyn McConachie (11)	152
Magen Donnelly (12)	152
Nicole Barrett (11)	153
Paul Stuart (11)	154
Gordon Bushby (11)	154
Martin Wright (12)	155
Connor Downie (11)	155
Nicole Fallon (12)	156
Joanne Walker (11)	156
Holly J McDougall (11)	157
Sophie McCullagh (11)	157
Shaughn Meechan (11)	158
Lisa McAdams (11)	158
Alix Hutcheson (11)	159
Natalie Lester (12)	159
Liam McLaughlin (11)	160
Dean Burnett (11)	161
Kyle Wands (12)	162
Jennifer Ann Calder (11)	163

St Francis Of Assisi Primary School, Cumbernauld

Eilidh McCadden (11)	163
Roisin Miller (11)	164
Michael Hamilton (10)	164
Andrew Doherty (11)	165
Daniel Rudden (10)	165
Roisin Donnelly (9)	166
Jacob McCann (9)	166
Alexandra Lawson (9)	167
Lisa Divers (10)	168

St Leonards Primary School, Dunfermline

Rüyana Rüzgar (9)	168
Lauren Gallagher (9)	168
Lisa Malpas (9)	169
Jack Adamson (8)	169
Samuel O'Brien (8)	169
Hayley Gibson (8)	170
Sean MacGregor (9)	170
Louis Wain (8)	170

Cameron Campbell (8)   171
Ashley Kendall (8)   171
Joeanne Nicol (9)   171
Emily Christie (8)   172
Claire Aitchison (8)   172
John Lessels (10)   172
Andrew Sherriffs (8)   173
Heather Dunn (8)   173
Mark Keir (9)   173
Liam Morton (8)   174
Brandon Bryce (8)   174
Chelsea Trotter (8)   174
Michael Kerr (8)   175

Sea View School, Kirkcaldy
Kieron Treanor (8)   175
Emily Doherty (7)   176
Holly Jones (8)   177
Nicholas Diston (8)   178
Hannah Wood (7)   179
William Dineen (8)   180
Danny Dineen (7)   181
Laura Innes (8)   182
Robbie Gavin (9)   183

Stoneywood Primary School, Aberdeen
Robert Sinclair (12)   183
Ross Soutar (11)   184
Ian Lawson (12)   184
Lewis Gary Taylor (12)   185

Torbain Primary School, Kirkcaldy
Brian Harley (10)   185
Sarah Fleming (9)   186
Robbie Balfour (10)   186

Townhill Primary School, Hamilton
Heather Moore (8)   186
Jessica Secmezsoy Urquhart (10)   186
Emma Gordon (10)   187

Lynsey Smith (10)   187
Emma Keir (9)   187
Nicola Wilson (10)   187
Kirsten Maclean (9)   188
Katie Fairfull (9)   188
Emma Caldwell (9)   188

The Poems

Little Puppies

Six little puppies going for a dive,
One of them jumped and then there were five.

Five little puppies sitting on the floor,
One went out the door then there were four.

Four little puppies, one saw a bee,
One of them went away and then there were three.

Three little puppies creeping round and round,
One went 'Boo' and then there were two.

Two little puppies eating a bun,
One got fat and then were was one.

One little puppy all alone,
He went away and then there were none.

Kimberley Stewart (8)
Alyth Primary School, Blairgowrie

Five Little Monkeys

Five little monkeys spinning round and round,
One fell on the floor, then there were four.

Four little monkeys going to the slope,
One went to ski, then there were three.

Three little monkeys each saying, 'Boo!'
One got scared, then there were two.

Two little monkeys lying in the sun,
One got burned, then there was one.

One little monkey all on his own,
He went to find his friends, then there were none.

Matthew McLauchlan (7)
Alyth Primary School, Blairgowrie

My Opposites

If I say fat
Will you say thin?
If I say long
Will you say short?

If I say mum
Will you say dad?
If I say granny
Will you say grandad?

If I say sister
Will you say brother?
If I say summer
Will you say winter?

Ian Fotheringham (8)
Alyth Primary School, Blairgowrie

The Little Seed

Here is a seed
And here is a flower
This one looks like it might flower
One is purple
One is pink
One's as big as a big white sink

Some are fat and some are thin
But certainly I will not give in
This one's short
And this one's tall
And this one looks like it might fall . . .

Rebecca Campbell (8)
Alyth Primary School, Blairgowrie

Six Little Dogs

Six little dogs found a hive
One got stung
And then there were five

Five little dogs found a door
One got so surprised
Then there were four

Four little dogs paid a fee
One got a letter
And then there were three

Three little dogs
One got a shampoo
And then there were two

Two little dogs found a bun
One got sick
And then there was one

One little dog
He went off to have some fun
And then there were none.

Eryn Sinclair (8)
Alyth Primary School, Blairgowrie

Food Is Good

Food is lovely, food is great
Food is tasty and delicious
I love melted chocolate
And banana drink

Food is lovely, food is great
It is lovely and tasty
I like spaghetti Bolognese
And tomato sauce.

Jake Seaward (8)
Banff Primary School, Banff

Food

I love food
Any kind of food
I like macaroni and cheese
Sugary sweets
And strawberries

If I am lucky
I get marshmallows
With chocolate sauce
I love bubblegum
And ice cream

Turkey, chicken
Or Christmas meals
What's the choice?
I do not know
Maybe altogether.

Abbey Yorkston (7)
Banff Primary School, Banff

Food

Apples are good for your teeth
How about trying an apple feast?

Pineapples are good
Some are spiky
They are tasty
Nice, juicy and good

Bananas are good
But you shouldn't eat the skin
Because you would get a sore belly.

Jamie Laing (7)
Banff Primary School, Banff

Food

Food is lovely
Food is great
I do like apple tart
It is delicious and scrumptious
Let's all have a mighty feast

Food is great
Food is lovely
I do like tomato soup
It is smashing
Let's all have a big meal

Food is lovely
Food is great
I do like chocolate cake
It is sweet and tasty
Delicious too.

Lauren Smith (7)
Banff Primary School, Banff

Food

Food, food, it's lovely and great,
Chicken and chocolate cake,
I love to eat toffee and sweets,
That are chewy and sour,
I love to eat, eat, eat.

Pears and kiwis are really juicy,
Strawberries and grapes are juicy too,
I would like to get an ice cream or two,
I love turkey, I love rice,
Dinner time is really nice.

Hattie Chisnall (7)
Banff Primary School, Banff

Food

Food is lovely, food is great
Let's all have a piece of steak
I like to eat, it's good for your health
Good for your body
It is sweet and tasty

Food is lovely, food is great
Let's all have a chocolate cake
It is yummy, nice and iced
It is just a tasty cake.

Alex Charlton (7)
Banff Primary School, Banff

Food

Food is delicious, food is good
I do love chocolate cake

Food is lovely, food is great
I always enjoy tomato soup

Food is yummy, food is great
It gives me energy.

Sarah Morrison (7)
Banff Primary School, Banff

Poem

There was a boy called Frank
Who put some fish in a tank
He went to bed
And ate some bread
When he got up the fish were dead.

Kieran Smith (10)
Banff Primary School, Banff

A Sleepy Spell

A slow-moving sloth
A towel or cloth
The slime of a snail
And the tail of a whale
The nose of a skunk
And an elephant's trunk

Burn, burn and burn some more
Hopefully this will make you snore

The wing of an eagle
The tongue of a beagle
Stir thoroughly
Until it goes whirly
A penguin's beak
And the turban of a Sikh

Burn, burn and burn some more
Hopefully this will make you snore!

Shaun Miller (11)
Banff Primary School, Banff

Food

Food is great, food I can't resist
Chocolate cake is the best
But you can't forget the rest
Double chocolate cookies
Is the one for me
I put it in my mouth in one gulp
Down to my stomach
I pinch the menu off the waiter's hands
And I look for hot dogs and cheeseburgers
Now I'm full up so I am ready to go.

James Robertson (8)
Banff Primary School, Banff

Spell

An eye of a frog,
A head of a rat,
The tongue of a dog,
The tail of a cat.

Hubble, bubble, double trouble
Make my cauldron bake and bubble

A horse's mane
A spider's web
A drop of rain
And a dead man's leg

Hubble, bubble, double trouble
Make my cauldron bake and bubble!

Lisa Davidson (11)
Banff Primary School, Banff

Evil Spell

Get a skeleton
Break the bones
Toss them in the cauldron
Hear them groan
Then stir it when it's boiled and baked

Double bubble boil and bubble
Fire flame and cauldron hubble

Get a head
Make sure it's dead
Then add a bit of lightning ray
As something evil comes this way.

Chelsea Page (10)
Banff Primary School, Banff

The Stars

The stars are coming out tonight
As they do every night
Reflected by the shining sea
The stars have made the galaxy

Constellations and shooting stars
They look tiny but are so far
Shooting stars make wishes too
And soon your wishes will come true

They make the night special
They make the night shine
They glint up in space
And fade at daytime.

Tara Copic (10)
Banff Primary School, Banff

A Toad Spell

Gather round the cauldron,
We will make a spell,
Add some ink, black as night,
You won't see a bit of light.

Watch the cauldron bubble,
It will soon cause trouble.

A baby toad,
From up the road,
A rat's tall,
Will not fail.

Watch the cauldron bubble,
It will soon cause trouble.

Jordan Cassie (11)
Banff Primary School, Banff

Summer Holidays

S ummer is the best time of the year
U p to 100 degrees
M y mum got sunburnt
M y dad went to tea in the park
E verybody was absolutely melting
R ain never came

H elp then came
O n Sunday it was very hot
L ots of people were eating ice cream
I was the one who was grounded
D ad went to Japan
A nd left me feeling bored
Y ou could have got sunburnt
S ummer is the best time of the year.

Jo Bruce (10)
Banff Primary School, Banff

Summer Holidays!

S ummer was hot
U tterly ace
M y brother moaned the whole time
M y mum enjoyed our holiday
E ven though it rained some days
R ain was the worst!

H olidays are really fun
O n Sunday we left for our holiday
L ovely weather came
I went to Stirling for my holiday
D ad had to put up the tent
A nd I just played
Y ippee!
S tirling was the best.

Shannon Smith (10)
Banff Primary School, Banff

Spaceship

S udden countdown as we prepare
P utting our harnesses on
A s we leave I say goodbye
C an you see us, we're in the sky?
E veryone cries as we go
S uddenly a blast as the thrust goes on
H urry up we're on our way
I hope I'm not here to stay
P romise I'll be back another day.

Steven Gallon (11)
Banff Primary School, Banff

Summer

S chool's out and summer's in,
U sually it's boring,
M y mum's going shopping,
M other Nature is waiting,
E veryone getting sunburnt,
R ats! Summer ends.

Jamie Douglas (10)
Banff Primary School, Banff

Rocket

R acing through the midnight sky,
O ver the clouds it does fly,
C rackling fire streaming behind it,
K ids and grown-ups watch it excited,
E verybody waving goodbye,
T o the astronauts flying high.

Kyle Jeffrey (11)
Banff Primary School, Banff

Hallowe'en

Hubble bubble let's make some trouble,
If you want, we'll make it double!

First scrape in a bird's legs,
Then chuck in a rusty peg.

Hubble bubble let's make some trouble,
If you want we'll make it double!

Next fling in a small trout,
Then put in a pig's snout.

Hubble bubble let's make some trouble,
If you want we'll make it double!

Now throw in a black bat's wing,
Then pour in a bumblebee's sting.

Hubble bubble let's make some trouble,
If you want we'll make it double!

Samantha Charlton (11)
Banff Primary School, Banff

Dreaming Of Space

Gliding through the darkness, high above the clouds
Stars shining like twinkling fairy lights, not making a sound
I can see the planets levitating in the air
Like giant glass marbles, spinning without a care
Back to Earth with a bump, in my ordinary bed
Not soaring or gliding but just lying there instead
But tomorrow night I will come back and look at the planets again
And maybe someday I'll see for real
But I'll keep on dreaming until then.

Amy Gordon (10)
Banff Primary School, Banff

An Evil Spell

Hubble bubble horrible trouble
How about we make it double?

First throw in a head of a bat
Then place in a tail of a cat

Hubble bubble horrible trouble
How about we make it double?

Now drip in a blind bee's sting
Followed by an owl's wing

Hubble bubble horrible trouble
How about we make it double?

Some spiders' webs to bind it well
Now I'm ready with my spell

Hubble bubble horrible trouble
How about we make it double?

Danielle Burrows (11)
Banff Primary School, Banff

Satellite

There's a satellite in the sky,
Taking photos of planets nearby.

Standing there on its own,
A huge piece of metal always alone.

Floating in orbit, day and night,
So bright; such a wonderful sight.

Hard to see from planet Earth,
Taking photos of the city of Perth.

Amanda Simpson (11)
Banff Primary School, Banff

A Spell

Light the fire in the night
Then put in some dynamite
Three snake tongues, two rotten eggs
Stir the cauldron till it's right

Twenty days and twenty nights
I'll make it come with all my might

Half of a snake
This is a piece of cake
Four eyeballs and a bit of cow
Stir it well and mix it now

Twenty days and twenty nights
I'll make it come with all my might.

Grant Thomson (11)
Banff Primary School, Banff

The Stars

The stars are coming out tonight,
As they do every night,
Reflected by the shining sea,
The stars have made the galaxy,
Constellations and shooting stars,
They look so tiny but are so far,
Shooting stars make wishes too
And soon your wishes will come true,
They make the night special,
They make the night shine,
They glint up in space
And fade at daytime.

Danielle McLeod (10)
Banff Primary School, Banff

Vikings

Vikings are huge and hairy
They are very good at fighting
They make sharp weapons
I think they are very scary

They like to invade day and night
And they like gold and silver
I hate Vikings because they are scary!
They are huge and they give you a fright

They are very bloodthirsty and mean
And I was very frightened
They are big like a monster
And they like to scream.

Staci Jeffrey (9)
Banff Primary School, Banff

Viking Poem

Vikings are very scary
And like to kill
They have huge bulging muscles
They have big beards and they are hairy

Vikings love to fight
The Vikings like to kill
They like to steal
They travel over stormy seas at night

Vikings like to raid
The Vikings are strong
They love to attack
The Vikings do not get paid.

Robyn Leask (9)
Banff Primary School, Banff

Spaceship

S paceships soaring through the sky
P eople waving a happy goodbye
A nd everyone witnessing a horrible sight
'C ause a spaceship just hit the meteorite
E verybody watching the big bash
S paceship covered in lots of ash
H appy people turning sad
I n the night still nobody was glad
P eople all remembering that terrible crash.

Gavin Leask (11)
Banff Primary School, Banff

Rocket

R ushing into space, flying high
O ver the moon and past the stars
C louds so small behind us
K eeping on track for Jupiter
E scaping the meteorites crashing towards us
T hundering past Mars onto Jupiter.

Sarah Johnston (10)
Banff Primary School, Banff

Rocket

R ising up above the ground,
O ver the skies they will be found,
C rackle and pop. They're king of the sky,
K eep your pets inside and watch fireworks fly,
E verybody comes to see,
T he fireworks fly over the trees.

Andrew Baxter (11)
Banff Primary School, Banff

Holidays!

H ot sun boiling in the sky
O tters clapping their fins
L ast day of your holidays, try to make it your best
I ce cream dripping all over your clothes
D olphins jumping in and out of the water
A nd no children to be seen in their houses
Y oung boys and girls playing in the street
S ummer holidays are the best.

Megan Allan (10)
Banff Primary School, Banff

Planets

P luto is the smallest planet
L ittle and round
A ll planets orbit the sun
N eptune is green and cold
E arth is the third planet from the sun
T he largest planet is Jupiter
S aturn has got three rings.

Daryl Scott (11)
Banff Primary School, Banff

Bonfire

B urning fire
O n the ground
N oisy fireworks make a sound
F ire blazing
I n the night
R ed fire burning bright
E verybody loves a bonfire in the night.

Dean Morison (10)
Banff Primary School, Banff

Viking Poem

Vikings are scary with their bloody teeth,
They look hairy and have lots of weapons
The Vikings will jump out of their long ship
And try to invade you, led by their chief.

The Vikings come to attack at night,
They love to kill with swords and axes.
They swish their big torch from side to side
And it might catch fire and set houses alight.

The Vikings took shiny money, jewels like rubies,
Slaves that are poor so they can build house
With no cupboards, with one room,
The Vikings didn't listen to rules!

Henna Khan (9)
Banff Primary School, Banff

Vikings

Bloodthirsty Vikings come to raid
They sail with their long ships over stormy seas
The Vikings have spears, axes and swords
And they might want to *invade!*

Viking farmers plough their fields
They take healthy food for families
Fierce Vikings like their meals
And they have lots of shields

With their huge muscles they work hard
They have very bushy beards
The Vikings come from Scandinavia
And they kill and steal!

Kennedy Duncan (8)
Banff Primary School, Banff

Viking Poem

Vikings are fierce and like to fight
They live with their families and travel at night
With their long ships
Then they attack at night

Vikings plant their fields
Vikings have big, hairy beards
On their farms they grow apples
And they use their axes to fight.

Jade Fraser (8)
Banff Primary School, Banff

Poem

Vikings loved to fight,
They used weapons to kill,
Spears, axes, swords and shields,
They liked to attack at night,
They came in long ships,
They went from place to place
With fire torches to see in the dark.

Adele West (8)
Banff Primary School, Banff

Vikings

Vikings like to fight
They are hairy and ugly
And they look scary with anger
They hunt at night.

Jordan Paterson (9)
Banff Primary School, Banff

Viking Poem

Vikings love to fight
And their weapons are dripping with blood,
They sail for miles and miles,
They could attack at the dead of night.

Vikings love to farm,
But some love to raid,
They can make lots of meats
And can also harm you.

They believe in the afterlife where all dead men are
Once you're dead they can't kill you with a knife again
You might have died because of disease
And they can't kill you again!

Vikings are mean and scary
They could trap you like a rat
And they would cook you in a fire pit
They are also very hairy!

Jennifer Bruce (8)
Banff Primary School, Banff

Vikings

Viking warriors travel in their long ships coming in to fight
They've got swords, axes and daggers to slit your throat
They have big bushy hair
They fight all night

They feast all night and sometimes fight all night and day
The Viking gods can hear them
They get very angry and *shout* at them
And rise from the dead to kill them.

Erin Sutherland (8)
Banff Primary School, Banff

The Vikings

The Vikings are fierce and they like to fight
They live with their family
And make sharp swords and axes
Some like to fight at night

The Vikings like to invade
They are so bloodthirsty
Their oars are so big
They like to think of raids

The Vikings tell sagas
They like to sail in stormy seas
They have bulging muscles
The children like to stay close to their mamas.

Vanessa Wood (9)
Banff Primary School, Banff

Viking Poem

Vikings are fierce and scary,
They row their long ships through the stormy seas
Vikings have massive bulging muscles
They like killing and fighting

Vikings like to raid
They came from Sweden, Denmark and Norway,
They have blood on their weapons,
Vikings like to invade.

Vikings like parrots,
Vikings have gardens,
Vikings plough their fields,
They like carrots.

Shaun Priest (8)
Banff Primary School, Banff

Viking Poem

Vikings are fierce and scary
Farming is one of their skills
They travel in long ships with massive oars
And their beards are hairy

They love to fight in a battle
And kill people with all their might
And cook over fire pits
They have feasts and eat cattle

Vikings love to raid
They always kill and hate
They travel in long ships
And also invade.

Bethan Coady (8)
Banff Primary School, Banff

Viking Poems

Vikings were fierce and scary,
They travelled in their long ships over stormy seas
And they had bushy hair
With beards that were hairy

Vikings love to fight
They live in Scandinavia and like to kill
Sometimes they raid in the dead of night

Vikings have gods of their own
They have the god Oden with one eye
And Thor, the god that has a hammer that can kill
They are never alone.

Jack Duncan (8)
Banff Primary School, Banff

Vikings

Viking warriors love to fight
In their long ships they sail to raid other countries
Waving their axes over their heads
A Viking life for me!
They will attack in moonlight

Vikings kills at the stroke of midnight
As soon as villagers wake up
They'll find their family dead on the ground
As sneaky as a cheetah
They will give you a fright

Vikings are head and mean
They are horrid from top to toe
They will attack you any day!
Just watch out for a boat, they will then raid.

Chloe Low (9)
Banff Primary School, Banff

Viking Poem

Vikings are very scary
With massive bulging muscles
They have pointy swords
Watch out, they are huge and hairy!

Thor is the god of thunder,
He rides on a chariot pulled by two giant goats
He likes fighting

I hate the north men
They kill people with their weapons
I think they are awfully scary
They killed a lot of brave men.

Scott Wilson (8)
Banff Primary School, Banff

The Toilet Made A Noise

On Friday night,
9pm,
The toilet made a noise,
I didn't like the sound of it,
So I just played with my toys,
But on Saturday night,
9pm,
The toilet choked a wheeze,
I didn't like the sound of it,
It was telling me to freeze!
I told my mum,
She said, 'Nonsense!'
So all I got for pocket money
Was 50 pence,
But on Sunday night,
9pm,
The toilet was asleep,
So I didn't have to go to bed
Wanting to cry and weep.

Laura Mathers (11)
Banff Primary School, Banff

Senses

A crocodile's jaws
Sound like a car crash
A crocodile looks like a sausage
A crocodile feels like football studs.

Luke Mackenzie (8)
Banff Primary School, Banff

Great Food

Food is great, I love cake,
It's brown, hot and round
I couldn't even share a bit of it
Tastes like chocolate spread
I eat it every day
So when I am hungry I just take a bite
It makes me feel like magic

I love pizza, it's yellow and crusty
When it's soft I'll just leave it
When it's hot it tastes so good
When it's cold it's still the same
Yum-yum pizza

Food is great, food is great
I'll just have a snack
A chocolate cake
A juicy apple
And a big snack for me.

Kelsie Haggerty (7)
Banff Primary School, Banff

Viking Poem

Vikings give you a fright,
They have axes, swords and shields
After they have killed
They sail on the stormy seas with their oars
Vikings have bulging muscles

Be careful 'cause they might attack in the night
Vikings are hairy
They sail on the sea with their long ships
They live in Norway, Sweden and Denmark
Sometimes they can be a bit scary!

Hilary McArthur (8)
Banff Primary School, Banff

Pretty Pebbles

Pretty pebbles on the shore,
Show me the blue ocean down below,
Show me the striped, coloured fish,
Show me the sharp, bubbly coral,
Show me your dark, hidden secrets,
Show me the bright sunshine through the water,
Show me each unique shell,
Show me the dusty ocean floor,
Show me the ocean's dangers,
Show me the sunset on the horizon,
Shoe me the pretty pebbles on the shore.

Shanna Yeats (11)
Bervie Primary School, Montrose

Sailing

Sailing in a tense race,
Continually wondering about your place,
Racing excitedly for the cup,
Family and friends wishing good luck,
The wind is starting to pick up
So we're not going to stop,
We're flying by the finish line
And the cup is mine!

Sean Tait (10)
Bervie Primary School, Montrose

The Bird

The swift bird flying high in the languid sky,
The bright, bright yellow
Sun shining through
Like an orange waiting to be picked.

Stuart Crockett (11)
Bervie Primary School, Montrose

Me!

I'm the best at writing stories
Because my stories are the fabbest in the universe.

I'm the best at singing
Because I'm better than an opera singer.

I'm the best at trampolining
Because I can jump right into space.

I'm the best at composing songs
Because my songs are better than Beethoven's.

I'm just brilliant aren't I?
I'm the greatest in the world!

Callum Ogilvie (11)
Bervie Primary School, Montrose

The Sun

The sun is the best thing the world has ever seen,
It's a fiery ball of lava that would burn you straight away
You have to have your sunlotion on
Or it will use its magic to burn you
It's like a reward when you do something good
The sun also bullies the water on the pavement
It's bigger than the Pacific Ocean.

Scott McKenzie (12)
Bervie Primary School, Montrose

The Football

It is a black and white rocket shot high into the summer sky
It is a gym that only me and my mates go to
It is a bullet shot like a missile in the sea
It is as round as the spherical sun
It is a flaming-hot ball shot through five brick walls
It keeps the blood pumping in my body.

Daniel Taylor (12)
Bervie Primary School, Montrose

Homework

I hate homework -
But sometimes it can be fun
'Oh! I'll do it later!'
'You will do it now!'
'I am going out,
See ya.'
I hate homework -
But it helps me in class
'Oh! I'll do it later!'
'You'll do it now.'
Too late
'Bedtime.'
'But Mum, my homework.'
'Mrs Ross won't be amused.'
'Why isn't your homework done?'
Shouted Mrs Ross.

Ashley Simpson (11)
Bervie Primary School, Montrose

My Kitten

My kitten is mad
But I hate it when she is bad
She creates destruction
But is as small as a bun
She is cute
But looks like a ball of soot
She is mayhem
But she sleeps in my den
She is nice
But I hope she doesn't eat mice
I love her as much as my other cat.

Daniel Robb (11)
Bervie Primary School, Montrose

My Cat, Teddy

My cat, Teddy didn't cost a pound
But to me he is priceless
He is always ready to pounce
He is as feral as a fierce tiger
When he's hunting
He's as quiet as a mouse
As wild as the wind
As fast as a leopard
As cunning as a fox
And as swift as an eagle
But when he's relaxed he's a cuddly kitten
I think he's the best pet I'll ever have
He is, in my eyes, *purrfect*.

Peter Harden (11)
Bervie Primary School, Montrose

My Daddy, David

My daddy, David
Is a wonderful man, he is a football lover,
He is my daddy, David.

My daddy, David
Can touch the stars,
He can eat a thousand hot dogs,
He is my daddy, David.

My daddy, David
Guides my path,
He leads my every step,
He is my daddy, David,
I love you Daddy.

Rebecca Metcalfe (12)
Bervie Primary School, Montrose

Spirit Of The West

He is as fast as the rushing river,
As strong as the wind,
As free as an eagle,
Swooping across the land,
His tangled raven mane flying in the wild wind,
As caring as a father to his son,
His name is Spirit,
He is the stallion of the cimeron herd.

Jacqui Kerr (11)
Bervie Primary School, Montrose

My Cat, Milly

Milly follows me all around the house
Creeping even quieter than a mouse
She always waits outside the bathroom door
Most of the time waiting for me
She even follows me downstairs
When I've been called for my tea
When I go to bed I cuddle her like my ted
I love my cat Milly
But sometimes she can be silly.

Amy Jamieson (10)
Bervie Primary School, Montrose

Warhammer Is . . .

Warhammer is as detailed as Celtic letters,
            as hard as a brick wall,
            but as fragile as glass.
Warhammer is as colourful as a rainbow,
            as fascinating as time itself.

Cameron Woodger (10)
Bervie Primary School, Montrose

Me

I'm the *best* at netball, because I can get the ball in the net
from the top of the court!

I'm the *best* at remembering things because I remember
when and what and don't forget!

I'm the *best* at history because I know when it happened!

I'm the *best* at chocolate eating because I'll eat
it whenever I want!

Lyndsay Jarvie (11)
Bervie Primary School, Montrose

My Big Brother

He's like a rocket zooming into outer space
He's a great big ape-man
Swinging from branch to branch
He never stops watching the amazing TV
If I turn it off
He starts running after me!
But he is my brother
And I do like him too -
When he's nice of course!

Gemma Lamb (10)
Bervie Primary School, Montrose

Me!

I am good at everything because I am just the best,
I play around all day and forget about the rest,
I go to the river and play all day,
That is good because my birthday is in May,
Yeah!

Becky MacQueen (10)
Bervie Primary School, Montrose

My Grandpa

My grandpa is as daft as a brush
He is an enormous tree standing in the garden
He likes to garden all the time
He never gets away from it
But when I'm up in Inverness
I drag him away.

Andrew Benton (11)
Bervie Primary School, Montrose

My Clerkhill School, Peterhead

Primary 1 was coming
And I was not a fool
I had so many choices
But I chose the Clerkhill School, Peterhead
One, because it's magic
Two, because it's cool
There's not a place quite like it
The super Clerkhill School, Peterhead.

Kyle Ritchie (8)
Clerkhill School, Peterhead

Kara

My sister's name is Kara
The babysitter is called Tara
She is supposed to look after her
But they just watch Harry Potter
She's not very tidy
A bit like a rotter
Taking all the time in the bath like an otter
Making lots of mess
That's my sister I guess.

Sean Henderson (9)
Clerkhill School, Peterhead

Old Mother Hubbard

Old Mother Hubbard went to the cupboard
To fetch her poor dog a bone
But when she got there the cupboard was bare
And her poor dog had none
She went to the fish shop
To get a cod
But when she came back
He was acting so odd.

Rosanne Borthwick (8)
Clerkhill School, Peterhead

My Sister, Emily

My sister is a twister
She goes up and down
She annoys me so much
I don't let her touch my stuff
She hates me and
She always eats my tea
My sis may be a pest
But I know she is simply
The best!

Gillian Tait (9)
Clerkhill School, Peterhead

My Brother, Ellis

My brother, Ellis is quite a menace
Every night and day,
He cries for his milk,
But it usually gets spilt,
But I love him anyway.

Joshua Ward (8)
Clerkhill School, Peterhead

My Big Sister

My big sister
Hates Brussels sprouts
She does not believe the rhyme they have
She is very annoying

She looks tall
She's taller than my mum
My family's got blue eyes just like her
And brown straight hair

Her hobbies are watching TV
But I do know what she likes
The CD *Pink*
She turns up the volume
She likes messy bedrooms

She likes to wear make-up
Sometimes plays jokes on me
She hits and kicks me
She changes the TV programme
She sometimes pulls out the TV plug

My big sister dislikes me
Sometimes she makes me cry
She doesn't like my video called 'Friends'.

Rachel Fakley (8)
Clerkhill School, Peterhead

Vampire

Vampire that says, 'Boo!'
Look at her creep out at night
Sucking people's blood
Saying boo to everyone
Werewolves under beds
Bats hanging from walls
We always sleep at sunlight
She hates garlic and crosses.

Jade Mair (8)
Clerkhill School, Peterhead

What's The Matter With Me?

When I was playing a game
My brother came
He destroyed the game
What a shame
He's a pain
When I was writing a song
My brother came along
He ripped the song and laughed at me
Why should he?
We began to fight!
My brother gave me a bite
I started roaring, 'Mum, I want you to come!'
My brother pretended to cry
My mum blamed me and gave a big sigh
What's the matter with me?

Eve Davidson (8)
Clerkhill School, Peterhead

There Was A Knight . . .

There was a knight
Who fought for a kite,
He had a fight,
In the middle of the night,
He got a fright
By a flashing light,
On his right
There was a height
Of delight,
By the crowd that had the light,
The knight went home
And started to moan
Because he got a fright.

Catherine Ritchie (10)
Clerkhill School, Peterhead

All About Laura Chalk

Laura likes ice cream and so do I, *yum yum yum*
She likes pets, I like them too, they're so cute
She loves her little sister, I think she's too cute
Laura hates work, I hate it more
She dislikes bullies and I hate them too
Her hobbies are skipping and swimming, *cool*
She is a nice girl, she has brown hair, brown eyes and she's very thin,
But she'll always be my best friend in the world.

Jennifer Rhynd (10)
Clerkhill School, Peterhead

My Dog, Penny

I have a dog called Penny
She is a Labrador retriever
She has golden hair and brown eyes
She always gets excited
She likes playing with her toys
She likes my sister and me.

Laura Chalk (9)
Clerkhill School, Peterhead

Love And Hate

What I hate about the jungle is that it is scary and wet,
What I love about a puppy is that it is cute and cuddly
What I hate about a crocodile is that it is scary and it bites
What I love about the sky is that it gives you light and it is blue
What I hate about my eyes is that they give me headaches
What I love about hospitals is that they care for people
What I hate about wasps is that they sting,
What I love about windows is that you can see out of them.

Lauren Mitchell (10)
Collydean Primary School, Glenrothes

It's Snowing

It's snowing
It's snowing
It's snowing all around

Jump on your sledge
And go down the hill

Play in the snow
And make your face glow

Make a snowman as big as you
I might even think it's you

Call on your friends, one and two

Come and play
Before the snow's away

It's time to go away for the night
But we'll be back in the morning.

Alex Marjoram (11)
Collydean Primary School, Glenrothes

Spooky Man

Spooky, spooky, spooky, you're freaking me right out
Who is that man behind me?
I'm getting scared right out!
He is getting closer
I need to walk fast or he will get me
I am hearing noises
I can't stand this now
He is right behind me
I need to run and hide
He is slowing down now
I'm going to run out of these woods.

Bradley Murray (10)
Collydean Primary School, Glenrothes

Up In Space

A is for aliens living up high.
B is for bumping right in the sky.
C is for creature first on the moon.
D is for dogs sleeping till noon.
E is for evil exploding the Earth.
F is for frightful mad doctor with girth.
G is for the grunting which aliens do.
H is for happy, we wish you were too.
I is for indigo Uranus dye.
J is for Jupiter, the one with an eye.
K is for kranky, not had much sleep.
L is for lantern to lead you through deep.
M is for Mercury close to the sun.
N is for Neptune not hot as a bun.
O is for orange, Saturn's ring.
P is for Pluto, the air is freezing.
Q is for quiet with no one up there.
R is for rocket zoom through the air.
S is for star ever so bright.
T is for tried to stay up all night.
U is for Uranus, too far to go to.
V is for Venus, miles to get to.
W is for wet Neptune's ground soon.
X is for exciting on the great big white moon.
Y is for not yet finished the case.
Z is for zonked, what a long day in space.

Stephanie Arnott (10)
Collydean Primary School, Glenrothes

Tigers - Haiku

Tigers in the grass
In the sun, yawning slowly
Thirsty as can be.

Emma Robertson (10)
Collydean Primary School, Glenrothes

Idol Acrostic Poem

A vril I like your clothes
V ery good at your songs
R ecord is long and good
I love your tops
L ong, long you are going to be famous

L ove your hair, very stylish
A nd I love everything about you
V oice is brilliant
I watch pop, you are on it and you are really good
G reat songs
N ever, ever go down
E ver, I will like you forever.

Kimberley Webster (8)
Collydean Primary School, Glenrothes

The Egyptians

T ravelling to Egypt on a plane
H urry up to catch a train
E nding up in a lost king tomb

E gypt is hot
G ot to water
Y ou will try to steal the Egyptian king daughter
P yramids to look at
T ombs to explore
I n the dark I walk
A nd I always hear spirits talk
N ot enough light for me to see
S ometimes I wish I was not here, *argh!*

Stuart Callison (10)
Collydean Primary School, Glenrothes

My Strange Family

My family is a strange wee bunch
with my sister and me exchanging a punch.
My dad's always lazing on the settee,
my mum's always tired cooking our tea.

My mum's always shouting
at the top of her lungs.
When she sees my sister's room
she well . . . shows off her tongue.

My dad is a chatterbox
when he comes home
because he's always watching footy
and he's always on the phone.

My sister is a pain,
an annoying little brat
but she is supposed to be clever,
cos her Chinese sign's the rat.

Oh and me well . . .
I'm just me!

Ashley Roy (11)
Collydean Primary School, Glenrothes

My Fat Cat

I have an adorable cat
Who is extremely fat
He would eat any type of food
Especially Whiskas, it is good
He purrs when he's brushed
And miaows when it's rushed
He plays with his toy mouse
Then runs wildly round the house
Finally he goes to bed
To rest his soft furry head
Eight hours away
Until he starts his busy day.

Michelle Proudfoot (10)
Collydean Primary School, Glenrothes

To A Lass

She looks at me with a beautiful face,
She's a lovely girl I would love to kiss,
I would love to give her all the world,
But she's given me a miss.

I gave her a rose,
But I stood on her toes,
She got really mad,
She gave me a slap.

She's really the only one for me,
My life was dull until she came,
She thought I was lame,
But now we're the same.

I am really head-over-heels for her,
We are very good friends for now,
I never want to ruin that,
So I think it is better like this.

Douglas Gold (12)
Collydean Primary School, Glenrothes

Habits

Habits, habits
I have bad habits
Slamming the door
Screaming at the boys
Talking to my teddies
Shouting at my mum
Saying, 'I hate my brother!'
Talking to my dad
Wondering where I am
Habits
Why do I have them?
I don't know how talking to my dad
Is a bad habit, oh well!

Megan Rutherford (10)
Collydean Primary School, Glenrothes

Fireworks

Bright, banging fireworks sparkling in the sky
Banging bright above people's heads
While the rest push to see making metal barriers go clanging
People cheering, people clapping the bright banging fireworks
Entertaining us happily as we watch with amazement
The fireworks going bang, crack, brightly in the night

Our tradition to Guy Fawkes is why we have it
So we cheer in the night with rockets over our heads
When they are in the sky they try to make us happy
And not to make all the babies who come cry
All along the show of the bright banging fireworks

Among us all our ears hear the sound of them happily in the sky
To let us remember Guy Fawkes.

Kevin Kerr (10)
Collydean Primary School, Glenrothes

Love And Hate

What I love about dogs is they are sweet and cuddly.
What I hate about dogs is they are very noisy.
What I love about cats is they let you hold them and they
let you cuddle them.
What I hate about cats is they bite you and scratch you.
What I love about ferrets is they lick you.
What I hate about ferrets is they bite you when you try to
play with them.
What I love about mice is they are so small and cute.
What I hate about mice is they only live for about two years.
What I love about cheetahs is they have black spots.
What I hate about cheetahs is they can eat you.

Danni McGough (10)
Collydean Primary School, Glenrothes

My Best Friend

A best friend can be many things
But mine is better than them all
He is loyal and trustworthy
He is like a helping hand
Who will always be there

Sometimes we sway from our path of friendship
But we always get back on track
My best friend feels like an immovable ally
He looks like a hero
He sounds like a hundred horns
Heralding the dawn of the horizon

He is like a brother, never growing up
His words are like reassuring messages
Thrown from Heaven itself
The sound of his footsteps hits my ears
Like birds sounding the beginning of a new day
He is like a diary that talks
He is like a personal advice giver.

Josh Mills (10)
Collydean Primary School, Glenrothes

Friendship

I want to be friends with you till the sun stops shining in the sky
And till the wind is whistling all night
And when the moon is shining on the water at night

You're my best friend
I'll never forget you because you're my best friend
And always will be
You asked me to play with you on my first day of school
And that's when we became best friends and always will be
I will remember that day for the rest of our lives
That's why we're best friends and always will be.

Laura Barrett (11)
Collydean Primary School, Glenrothes

Different

I've always been somehow different,
Always felt so left out, so distant.

Not many people realise that I'm there,
Even if I'm sitting next to them on a chair.

Sometimes the teacher gives a shout,
Tells me to leave the room, to get out.

When I come home I rush to my room,
Hoping my parents will come home soon.

In the end they don't come home at all,
Even when I give them a call.

Now I feel so alone,
That all my skin is chilled to the bone.

No one ever gives a care,
Even if they do, it's very rare.

When my parents came home, at me they boomed,
Now I'm sure I'm definitely doomed!

Rachael Smith (11)
Collydean Primary School, Glenrothes

Glenrothes

G lorious Glenrothes
L ovely sights to see
E normous town park
N ice place to sit
R othes pit was flooded
O ur town in Scotland is the best
T he mines have all closed
H elp Glenrothes stay clean - recycle
E veryone should see the hills
S uper Glenrothes.

Sarah Campbell (8)
Collydean Primary School, Glenrothes

My Bedroom

In my bedroom lies my bed
On my bed sits my ted
In my bedroom neat and tidy
Oh I like to sleep on Friday

My bedroom is small
My bedroom is tall
My bedroom is all I need
The walls of my bedroom are all so smooth
As smooth as my wooden floor

At the end of my bedroom there is a window
So clear and clean
It glistens and shines in the morning light, so bright

Beyond my curtains hang my blinds
That block out the morning light of summer
I can clear my mind in my bedroom
Of the day that has passed by

In my bedroom I do all these things
From clearing my mind to making my bed
But the best thing I do in my room is . . .
Sleep, sleep, sleep!

Claire Pollock (10)
Collydean Primary School, Glenrothes

Fireworks

F ireworks are great
I really think they are
R ight, let's get the car started, let's not be late
E verywhere was crowded
W ow! A pound to watch
O h no, it's nearly started
R eally, I'm not kidding
K ites are not allowed today
S o can we stay all night?

Jessica Smith (10)
Collydean Primary School, Glenrothes

Bullying Poem

Bullying's bad
They think it's cool
You better watch out
They think they rule

Bullying is violence
You might get silence
You better run
And don't turn

You better tell
But don't get caught
The bully is near
So stay alert

Bullies should be charged
For all they have done
To see what it is like
To get a fright.

Nick Mitchell (11)
Collydean Primary School, Glenrothes

The Monsters

The monster under my bed
Keeps on banging his head
The monster in my cupboard
Is totally undiscovered
The monster looking out my window
Such a pity he is blind though
The monster slamming my door
Is making my head sore
The monster talking to me
Is called Blab-a-di-be
The monster on my bed
Always needs to be fed.

Marissa Kennedy (10)
Collydean Primary School, Glenrothes

My Best Friend

O' ma best friend is caring and kind,
She's always giving me a bit o' her mind,
She will always be ma best friend,
Until our friendship comes tae an end.

We share and bear our problems t'gither,
We will be friends forever and ever,
She makes me laugh and giggle with glee,
An awfy guid friendship I really can see.

Kirsty Cheape (11)
Collydean Primary School, Glenrothes

Secrets

Through the wood and over the hill
There's a lot of secrets still to tell
In every tree in every leaf
They hold a tale, story or even a secret

For every word you should listen
Before they let you through
In the river, over the mountain, wherever
There's a lot of secrets still to tell.

Luke Beimers (12)
Collydean Primary School, Glenrothes

My Cat

My cat is so greedy
He eats my mum's dinner
He comes in the house all wet
When he comes in we have to mop the floor
He is now on a diet because he is fat
He gets four packets of food a day and some treats
He also gets some milk and water just for him
Then he goes out again.

Stacey Clark (10)
Collydean Primary School, Glenrothes

My Bedroom

My bedroom is messy, it's full of junk
I'm always getting told to tidy it up
I like it that way, I don't like tidy
My bedroom is messy and I like it that way

It has a lamp and has a shelf
I have toys lying everywhere
I like it that way, I don't like it tidy
My bedroom is messy and I like it that way

Put that away, put this away
You have to do this, you have to do that
I like it that way, I don't like it tidy
My bedroom is messy and I like it that way

I'll tidy this up, I'll tidy that up
No Mum don't do that
I like it that way, I don't like it tidy
My bedroom is tidy and I hate it that way.

Rebecca Robb (9)
Collydean Primary School, Glenrothes

Cat's Eyes

There is a cat right outside my window,
It keeps looking at me everywhere I go,
I am outside playing
And the cat just sits there on the wall looking at me
I run into my house and look out my window,
But the cat just looks back at me
I don't know why, I don't know why
That cat's big green eyes just look back at me
It's night-time and the cat is away
I take one more look just to make sure
But it is there again sitting on the wall.

Jodie McKellar (10)
Collydean Primary School, Glenrothes

Nature

Hiding in the darkness,
Under the great oak tree,
Looking in all the wild places,
Busy as a bee.

Up the hills and mountains,
At the very top,
It might be an old volcano,
So watch it doesn't pop.

Standing near the loch,
Lapping against the rocks,
All the salty water,
Step out, don't wet your socks.

On the sands at the beach,
Tossing a ball in the air,
Buying an ice cream for 50p,
Now that price is very fair.

Deep down in the valley,
Only a few drops of water lie,
Birds swooping from the rocks,
Especially that magpie.

Now all this nature comes
From the great God in the sky,
He will look after you,
Until the day you say goodbye.

Lisa Proudfoot (12)
Collydean Primary School, Glenrothes

Bottlenose Dolphins - Haiku

Bottlenose dolphins
Squealing, clicking and diving
An ocean playground.

Phoebe Brown (10)
Collydean Primary School, Glenrothes

Friends

Friends are fun
Friends are great
Friends are cool
Friends are trustworthy
Friends are full of laughter

Friends play cool games
Friends have loads of sleepovers
Friends are kind
Friends have loads of cool toys
Friends are full of laughter

Friends are friendly
Friends are helpful
Friends tell good jokes
Friends should never break up
Friends are full of laughter

Friends are great when they smile
Friends are bad when they frown
Friends are good fun
Friends are funny
Friends are full of laughter.

Gemma Grieve (9)
Collydean Primary School, Glenrothes

Birds And Butterflies

It was a lovely summer's day
And I decided to go out to play,
I looked around and soon spotted
Some lovely butterflies, all of them dotted
And up above there were birds in a flock,
I stared at them, nearly tripping on a rock,
Then I came out of my dream, back to today,
But all the butterflies had gone away!

Lindsey McKerrell (8)
Collydean Primary School, Glenrothes

Hidden Treasure

Running through the night trees
Glowing eyes looking at me
Then a cat miaowed at me
Then a big booming bark
I ran and ran
Then I came out with a frightened face
In front of me was a big glowing castle
I ran up to the door
And it opened automatically
In front of me was a big brass door
It opened with a big bang
There was a piece of gold
I just looked at my watch
It was almost teatime
So I had to go
But I'll be back tomorrow.

Warren Gibson (10)
Collydean Primary School, Glenrothes

Winter Weather

Cauld, wat an' win's too,
Feelin' fine then so cauld,
Snow starts tae fa',
Ye git her gloves on'e,
Pick it up then ye throw.

Set tae row tae mak a snawman,
Ye think it's fun till ye drop,
Go inside tae git some het,
Nae mare fun till ye change.

Go back oot, it's tae deep,
Snaw goes in yer wellie bit,
It's awfy cauld, ye need tae go,
Ye go in, yer nice an' warm.

Carrie Deavin (11)
Collydean Primary School, Glenrothes

Love And Hate

I love McDonald's
But I hate Pizza Hut
I like Burger King and KFC
But I hate a Chinese and fish and chips
I like sports and the sea
But I hate school and reading
I like parks and swimming
But I hate fruit and vegetables
I like sweets and drinks
And hate fussy people
I like friends and family
But I hate bullies
I like cars and bikes
But I hate vans and lorries
I like buses and tree swings
But I hate barbed wire
I like water
But I hate fish
I like big houses
But I don't like little houses
I like balls
But I hate cricket bats.

Aaron Campbell (9)
Collydean Primary School, Glenrothes

Emotions

When I am happy, I feel as free as a bird
When I am moody, I won't speak a word
When I am angry, I cuddle up tight
When I'm surprised, it's because I got a fright!

When I'm delighted, I jump in the air
When I am grumpy, I feel life is unfair
When I am sad, I feel like a jar of lemon curd
When I am happy, I feel as free as a bird!

Rebekah Brown (11)
Collydean Primary School, Glenrothes

Fear

My fear is dark as midnight
It smells like a dead blood river
The river runs through my bedroom
I see dead bodies floating by me

When I look out my window
I hear the wind and it sounds like ghosts flying about the graveyard
When I am sleeping in my bed
I can hear a scream in the night

When I am in my bed
I can hear creaks coming towards me
I have nightmares about ghosts coming to haunt me
And take me to the haunted house

When I look out my window
I hear the wind and it sounds like ghosts flying about the graveyard
When I am sleeping in my bed
I can hear a scream in the night

Who's that tapping at the window?
Who's that knocking at the door?
Someone's tapping at the window
Someone's knocking at the door

A ghost was tapping at the window
A vampire was knocking at the door
They've come to haunt me.

Aimee Husband (9)
Collydean Primary School, Glenrothes

A Vacuum Cleaner

A moaning monster tied to the wall,
It eats everything in my room or the hall,
It silences everything, it always talks,
It has two wheels, it has no feet to walk,
It cleans like a maid but my mum has to help,
It swallowed some money and I gave a *yelp!*

Helen Bashforth (11)
Collydean Primary School, Glenrothes

The Seasons

Winter
In the winter you play in the snow
It's very cold you know
You can build a snowman or a snow-chair
I made one last year, it wasn't really strong

Spring
Now comes spring
You see all the buds
Sometimes in the morning they wake me up
On weekdays when I see animals I clap them going to school

Summer
And then we come to summer
I just can't wait until the holiday
I might just go to Turkey or even go to Spain
I really hope it's Jamaica
The sun will shine so bright
I might just turn brown
And it won't be a pretty sight

Autumn
Last of all is autumn
The trees are going bare
All the leaves are going red and some are even gold
I think I'm going to scream
I think they're going to poison me
Next they will go pale or blue
Or even like a barbeque.

Louise Leslie (10)
Collydean Primary School, Glenrothes

The Beach

The sun is shining
The waves are rushing
The sand is blowing
The shells are shiny
The stones are smooth

Everyone having picnics
Playing around
Swimming in the sea
Making sandcastles

Now it's time to go
Packing up the car
Everybody get in
Let's play a game 1, 2, 3

Nearly home
Let's play outside
In the swimming pool
It will be just like at the beach
Except we're in the garden 1, 2, 3

Splash, splish, splosh
In the water we go
Splash, splish, splosh
In the water we go

Playing with each other 1, 2, 3
Oh no, time for tea!
Quickly, let's hide 1, 2, 3
Here they come, ssh!

Oh no, they've found us, let's go
I wonder if we can play
This again tomorrow? 1, 2, 3.

Kelsey Sloane-Pirrie (10)
Collydean Primary School, Glenrothes

My Toys

I have lots of toys
Mine are not for boys
Sometimes I play with them outside
Or at the seaside
I've got rabbits, kangaroos, mice, dogs and cats
But I only have one or two rats
Some are pink
Some stink
One is called Dizzy
Another is called Frizzy
Some are white
Some are bright
They like to go into a tent
When it's for rent
Most are fluffy
The others are scruffy
A few are tall
Others are small
But I really do love them all.

Emily Reid (10)
Collydean Primary School, Glenrothes

The Bull

Fierce, big, it was ferocious,
I saw it charging at the old gate,
It soon broke free,
I felt the breath of a mean bull,
Meanly staring in my eyes,
Hearing its hooves stamping on the moist ground,
I can taste the horrible taste of a mean bull, not nice at all,
Smells like a bullet being shot right through me,
That bull that charged through the old fence,
It is now dead but I remember that day,
Clear as a cloud . . .

Sam Randall (9)
Collydean Primary School, Glenrothes

My Best Friend

My best friend is small and thin
My best friend has a very cheesy grin
My best friend has quite long hair
My friend always has her hair up
My friend has long eyelashes

My best friend loves to laugh
My best friend never forgets things
My friend is always talking
My best friend has brown hair
My best friend has never fallen off her chair

My friend tells me everything
My best friend keeps all my secrets
My best friend loves to play games
My friend can write really fast
My best friend loves being in the dark

My best friend and I have the same pencil case
My friend loves to draw
My best friend loves animals
My best friend has two annoying brothers
But that is why she is my best friend.

Kirsten Clunie (9)
Collydean Primary School, Glenrothes

My Emotions Poem

When I'm surprised, my eyes are like stars
But when I'm angry, I feel behind bars
When I'm delighted, my heart's filled with joy
But when I'm grumpy, I feel like hitting a boy
When I'm frightened, I crouch to the ground
But when I'm moody, I'm out of bounds
When I'm sad, my eyes fill with tears
But when I'm happy, I feel like a jumping deer.

Rhianne Pye (11)
Collydean Primary School, Glenrothes

Drugs

It sounds like thousands of doors groaning
And creaking in the wind
It looks like a prison that will never let you out
It demolishes all your happy thoughts
It drives you crazy with all these bad things
It takes over your mind and soon your body
Then you don't know what you're doing
You get addicted
You need more and more
You lose your job
You lose your family
It takes over you
You begin to steal money to buy it
You lose control of your life
Your life begins to revolve around drugs
You can't get out
It won't leave you alone
This is what drugs do to you.

Katy Horsburgh (10)
Collydean Primary School, Glenrothes

The 1st December

I have tae go tae work the day
Even though I'm tired
Have to show, I can't be late
Or else I will get fired

I try tae start ma engine
An' now am in a rush
The engine willnae start again
I'm no walkin' in slush

Ma boss is gonnae be so mad
But now I've just remembered
A cannae believe how daft I am
'Cause it's ma holidays in December.

Johnny Campbell (11)
Collydean Primary School, Glenrothes

Dogs

When you first get a dog they're always a nuisance
They are brown or black
You have to buy dog toys
When you do they're always everywhere
You also have to name them
When you buy dog toys they leave them everywhere
And they moult and there is dog hairs everywhere
They have floppy ears or hard ears
You might not even know they are there if they are floppy
If they bite, they have to have a nuzzle
But if they don't, you can leave it off
If they need a walk you can take them to the reservoir
They have to have their leads on though
Sometimes their leads are chains and sometimes they aren't
They bark and they growl
And they have sharp claws.

Carolanne Campbell (9)
Collydean Primary School, Glenrothes

The New Teacher

It's the first day back at school today
I just can't wait to get out to play
We're getting a new teacher, oh no!
There's the bell, c'mon let's go!

She strides in with a bin on her head
She's so white it looks like she's dead
I have a test for you to do
She drew her hanky and sneezed *atishoo!*
It seemed like we were in there for hours
She watched eating chocolates she devours

Tring! We were saved by the bell
She said, 'Boy wasn't that swell?'

Rebecca Edmonston (10)
Collydean Primary School, Glenrothes

Never Stare At A Grizzly Bear

You can stare at a teddy bear;
Glower and glare without a care
But it's only fair to make you aware
That a grizzly bear is a different affair.

Yes, a grizzly bear is a different affair,
Friendly ones are fairly rare,
Believe me then when I declare,
If you bump into its lair
Or trap it in a pit or similar snare
Or it eats your porridge or breaks your chair,
All I can say is you'd better beware,
Prepare yourself for a scary affair,
That'll probably turn out to be a proper nightmare
And it only takes one careless stare.

It only takes one careless stare
To make it mad and drive it spare,
Cos a bear cannot bear a human stare
And worst of all is the grizzly bear,
With claws that rip and slash and tear,
That's the grizzly truth, the grizzly truth,
The grizzly truth I swear,
For your own welfare, best gaze elsewhere,
Like over here or over there,
Directly down at your leather footwear
Or up at the weather in the wind-blown air,
Don't dare to stare at a grizzly bear,
Cos a bear can't bear a human stare
And worst of all is the grizzly bear,
It snorts and snarls, its nostrils flare,
You haven't got a hope, you're beyond despair.

Trudy Hamilton (9)
Collydean Primary School, Glenrothes

Friendship

I want to be friends with you
Till the swing stops swinging and the park has died
And we can go on till the birds can't fly
We can go on till the acorns stop cracking
And the world stops spinning and we die

If we are friends I will be your best friend forever and ever
I will be kind to you, very kind
I will protect you so you can not get hurt inside and outside

I will give you help, I will give you money to keep
I will give you company
I will give you laughter
And you will keep that laugh in your bucket

I will like you more than my brother
I like you more than my other friends
I like you more than the boys
And I like you more than apple juice and Coca-Cola.

Rebecca Forbes (11)
Collydean Primary School, Glenrothes

Mi Best Friend

Mi best friend makes me laugh,
Maks me giggle and maks me jiggle,
She's kind and caring, I couldnae choose a better friend
Mi best friend Micky

She looks after ye and sticks up for ye
She'll cheer ye up when you're doon
She'll never mak ye sad
Mi best friend Micky.

Danielle Woodford (12)
Collydean Primary School, Glenrothes

My Idol Poem

Friendly man
Expert football player
Runs very fast
Nobody can beat him
A very, very good player
Nobody can stop him because he is the best
Done all his stuff that he has been told to do
Better than any other player
Resting on the bench until he gets a shot
Incredible player
Clever player
Kicks the ball like an expert player
See him play
Everybody likes him
Never try to tackle him.

Jack Robb (8)
Collydean Primary School, Glenrothes

School

That horrible place called school
For those who act like a fool
For people who love to drool
And usually think it's cool

That disgusting place where people moan
From a distance you hear them groan

This is the place where children are blown with anger

The teachers are the worst of all
They pull your ear until it's impossible to hear
And you're staggering with fear.

Sean McGrath (11)
Collydean Primary School, Glenrothes

Sport Is Fun

My name is Dennis
Hockey is my game
I like playing tennis
It's not so lame

Badminton is good
Running is great
Eat healthy food
Run with a mate

Skating is nice
Blading rules
Playing on the ice
It's not for fools

Biking on the dirt
Going over bumps
I got hurt
Doing some jumps.

Graeme Marnie (11)
Collydean Primary School, Glenrothes

Emotions

When I am happy, I'll jump over the moon
When I am sad, I'll sit in the gloom
When I am surprised, I won't lie
When I am frightened, I stay in bed
When I am excited, it's like Christmas
When I am angry, it feels like Monday
When I am moody, it's hard to be nice
When I am filled with joy, I'll never annoy
When I am grumpy, you'll sigh
When I am happy, I'll jump over the moon.

Andrew Whiteley (11)
Collydean Primary School, Glenrothes

I like/I Hate

What I like about my friend is she's funny.
What I like about Labradors is that they are cute.
What I hate about dancing is that it's embarrassing.
What I like about custard is that it's yummy.
What I hate about clubs is that you mostly dance.
What I like about gymnastics is that you learn new things
What I hate about chocolate is that it makes me full.
What I hate about football is that it's dangerous.
What I hate about the moon is that it's shiny.
What I hate about vegetables is that they taste bad.
What I like about skating is that it's cool.
What I hate about work is that it's hard.

Bruce Campbell (10)
Collydean Primary School, Glenrothes

Love And Hate

What I love about animals is they are sometimes fluffy
What I hate about bears is they bite your head off
What I love about dogs is when they play with you when you are bored
What I hate about cats is they stink all the time
What I love about crocodiles is they have blood-red teeth
What I hate about fish is when you have to clean the tank
What I love about chicken is they taste good.

Charlie Campbell (11)
Collydean Primary School, Glenrothes

Mountains Of Thunder - Cinquain

So smart
And beautiful,
Oh mountains of thunder,
Catherine wheels and Roman candles,
Brilliant!

Sara Ward (11)
Collydean Primary School, Glenrothes

Our Class

Our class is very mad
The girls are sweet but
The boys are bad
There are two girls who are all alone
They are the bossy ones, the queens of the throne
But when they are bad, they get thrown out of the class
Straight through the window, smashing the glass
There is a boy called John Douglas
He's the classroom fool
Although he drives the teacher mad, he thinks he's really cool
Now our rhyme has come to an end
There's nothing to do for the teacher who's
Completely round the bend.

John Douglas (12)
Collydean Primary School, Glenrothes

Best Friends

B eing with my friends is fun
E ating chocolate with all of them
S aturday nights making a den
T elling jokes all day long

F reedom from our parents
R iding on our bikes
I n and out
E very day having fun hoping our friendship will
N ever end
D riving each other insane
S aturday we still are friends.

Ryan McNeill (10)
Collydean Primary School, Glenrothes

There's A Burglar In My House

There's a burglar in my house
It might just be a mouse
I hear a noise in the kitchen
It's probably just our pigeon
I've heard enough, it's time to go
Around the house with my dog, Mo
I see something coming up the stairs
What to do, do you know?
At last I know who it is
It's just my sister with a face like fizz
I'm off to bed now, see you later
I hope you don't turn into a gater.

Kyle Farmer (11)
Collydean Primary School, Glenrothes

It's Snawin' The Nicht

It's snawin' the nicht
Wi the wind blowin' through
Am wearin' twa jumpers
But ma nose is turned blue

It's snawin' the nicht
It's fair comin' doon
Those white fluffy snawflakes
Have hidden the moon.

Kayleigh McGough (12)
Collydean Primary School, Glenrothes

Flash Crash

Bang, bang
Lovely colours
Fireworks are going off
They are beautiful in the sky
Flash, crash.

Michelle Laing (10)
Collydean Primary School, Glenrothes

Silly Name Games

A is for Alex, whose shoes do not fit
B is for Barney, still he can't sit
C is for Caron, kind of a pain
D is for Daniel, he is insane
E is for Erika, she cannot spell
F is for Freddie, ran and he fell
G is for Georgina, sister of George
H is for Henry, plays on the gorge
 I is for Ilexa, likes her X-rays
J is for Jack, he's been sick for days
K is for Kane, mad at lunchtime
L is for Logan, silly all the time
M is for Monica, she drives me insane
N is for Nicky, lives down the lane
O is for Oliver, house number 12
P is for Patrick, he punches himself
Q is for Queen, don't know about this one
R is for Rita, has so much fun
S is for Sam, as silly as can be
T is for Tim, he's as silly as me
U is for Urwin, don't know if it's how to spell it
V is for Veronica, her torch just lit
W is for Wayne, he loves bonbons
X is for if you don't know how to spell your name
Y is for Yvonne, it's a French name
Z is for Zach, great friend of Wayne.

Logan Watt (10)
Collydean Primary School, Glenrothes

Black Banana

There was a girl called Hannah
Who sat on a black banana
Her favourite dress
Got in a mess
And she had to go in her pyjamas.

Hayley Burnett (8)
Collydean Primary School, Glenrothes

Emotions

When I am happy, I always glow
When I am sad, I'm as cold as snow
When I am joyful, I feel I can fly
When I am angry, I want to cry
When I am frightened, I feel really cold
When I am moody, I feel so bold!
When I am excited, I jump around
When I am grumpy, I sit on the ground
When I am happy, my smile shows.

Samantha Morgan (11)
Collydean Primary School, Glenrothes

Brown Deer

I was a big brown deer
I was really near
And I saw it had fear in its eyes
I then went near to have a peer
And saw it had a tear in its eye
I said, 'Do not fear
I will leave you here
To live year after year
As free as the wind goes by.'

Lucy Metcalfe (10)
Collydean Primary School, Glenrothes

Fireworks Are Brilliant

Fireworks sizzling
Sparkling, shooting
Spilling, whistling
Squealing, lighting
Glistening, whoosh!
Fireworks.

Farhan Ahmed (10)
Collydean Primary School, Glenrothes

Silly Names

A is for Aron who does not sit.
B is for Brendan whose shoes do not fit.
C is for Claire who's off her head.
D is for Danni who lost her bed.
E is for Emily who likes toad in the hole.
F is for Fiona who was home alone.
G is for George who took a fit.
H is for Henry who wants to sit.
I is for Ian who does swing.
J is for Jamie who does not swim.
K is for Kayleigh who fights a lot.
L is for Lucy who blights non-stop.
M is for Mary who might be big.
N is for Nicky who wears a wig.
O is for Oliver who eats non-stop.
P is for Peter who fights a lot.
Q is for Queen who cannot fight.
R is for Robert who doesn't know a thing about lights.
S is for Steven who never has shoes.
T is for Tammy who says lost as in lose.
U is for Ursula who never gets lots.
V is for Vicky who said 10p is a good cost.
W is for Wilma who says animals are animals.
X is for Xavier who says mammals are mammals.
Y is for Yevon who likes meatballs
Z is for Zack who has lots of footballs.

Jemma Black (10)
Collydean Primary School, Glenrothes

Fireworks - Cinquain

Bang, boom
Green, white, purple
Flashing, light up the sky
Zooming whistle in the air, bang
Flash, flash.

Kyle Maguire (10)
Collydean Primary School, Glenrothes

Emotions

When I am excited, I like to run around
But when I am moody, I stamp on the ground
When I am surprised, my eyes glow up
But when I am frightened, I get the hiccups
When I am delighted, I will be everyone's friend
But when I am grumpy, I will drive you round the bend
When I am like Santa, I'm full of joy
But when I am angry, I will hit all the boys
When I am sad, my eyes fill with tears
But when I am happy, I forget all my fears.

Danielle McSherry-Schee (12)
Collydean Primary School, Glenrothes

Fireworks

Fireworks soaring through moonlit sky
Will they explode or will they die?
The explosion is louder than I thought
Whoosh, zoom, fizz and *kabang*
Catherine wheels spinning magnificently
Beautiful, dazzling, twisting and turning
Rustling, going faster than anything I've seen.

Christopher Mackay (11)
Collydean Primary School, Glenrothes

Fireworks Bang! - Cinquain

Flashing,
Cool, fierce fireworks,
Shooting, zooming, whistle,
Ferocious, screeching, whoosh, clatter,
Fireworks!

Shannon Blackwood (10)
Collydean Primary School, Glenrothes

I Like/I Hate

What I like about friends is they are funny
What I like about Labradors is that they are cuddly
What I hate about dancing is that you get sore feet
What I like about custard is that it is tasty
What I hate about clubs is that they are dangerous (golf clubs)
What I like about gymnastics is you get fit
What I hate about chocolate is that I don't like nuts
What I hate about football is that I like it so much
What I like about the moon is that the moon makes me sleepy
What I hate about veg is it is disgusting.

Ross Jeffrey (10)
Collydean Primary School, Glenrothes

Emotions

When I am happy, I have a gleam in my eye
When I am sad, I begin to cry
When I am joyful, I begin to skip everywhere
When I am angry, I look like a devil
When I am delighted, I glow like the moon
When I am frightened, I cuddle into a ball
When I am surprised, I run into a big wall
When I am moody, I crush up a stuffed toy
When I am excited, I dance everywhere I go
But when I am happy, I have a gleam in my eye.

Stephanie Hopkins (11)
Collydean Primary School, Glenrothes

A Tropical Dream - Haiku

Somewhere far away
Where the deep blue sea glistens
The coconuts lay.

April Lavelle (11)
Collydean Primary School, Glenrothes

Scooby-Doo

Scooby-Doo
Can you hear him saying, 'Boo!'
He's running everywhere
With his hands in the air

Daphne's here
With her phone to her ear
She's got her pink dress
But her hair's just a mess

Shaggy's here
He's screaming with fear
Looking for Scooby-Doo
But all he heard was a ghost saying, 'Boo!'

Freddie is here
Without any fears
He's not screaming
Because he's dreaming

Scrappy's here
He's chasing away his fears
He fell on his head
And he thought he was dead.

Vanessa Gordon (11)
Collydean Primary School, Glenrothes

Fireworks! - Cinquain

Fireworks
Flash, bang, there look
Here, there and everywhere
Sparklers and there, look over there
Boom, bang.

Natasha Clugston (10)
Collydean Primary School, Glenrothes

Sport

My name is Paul
I like playing football
It's not so lame
It's just a game

Football is great
I play it with my mates
It is not just a fate
Just 'cause you lose
Don't hate

Running is great
I'm running to the gate
And I'm running everywhere
Like the day is never there.

Lorraine Brown (11)
Collydean Primary School, Glenrothes

Love Is . . .

Love is the air,
That runs without a care,
Love is the stare that I stare,
Love is the cake's solid layer.

Love is what family is about,
Love is not about falling out,
Love is the teacher letting me shout,
Love is not about being a lout.

Love is not running,
Love is letting people say what they say,
Love is doing things your own way,
Love is letting the consequences pay.

Shannon Smith (11)
Collydean Primary School, Glenrothes

Friendship

I want to be friends with you
Until the sea turns multicoloured
Trees turn blue and
The grass grows so long that
It's in space

If we are friends I will
Share my sweets and toys
Let you stay over and
Help you with your homework
And study with you

I will give you presents on your birthday and Christmas
Attention too, my time to listen to you
When you're upset and help you when you're sick

I will like you more than the world
My favourite food
My sister, my family
My football team I support
And my friends
And cheese and tomato pizza.

Amy McAteer (11)
Collydean Primary School, Glenrothes

Spring Is Here

Squirrels frolicking
Nuts and berries on the ground
Being eaten by the birds

Slimy, slithering snake
Silently waiting in the grass
Waiting for a frog

Fluffy little chicks
Just hatched out the egg
Same size as a brick.

Grant Fenton (11)
Collydean Primary School, Glenrothes

The Dog I Found

The dog I found had big brown eyes, when my friend saw him
She began to cry, 'It's so cuddly and furry,' said she,
Is it a she or is it a he?
His collar says Max, to the police we have sent a fax,
We fed him some dog food, he gobbled it right up,
We gave him some water, he drank it in a rush,
The police arrived and said, 'Where's the dog, Max?'
I said, 'You obviously got our fax.'
They took him home, he was now safe and sound,
I'll always remember the way he did bound.

Stasi Brogan (10)
Collydean Primary School, Glenrothes

When I Am . . .

When I am happy, I jump for joy and look at my ranger poster
When I am sad, I get very angry and spray-paint my walls
                                                with deodorant
When I am grumpy, I am very moody with everyone
When I am delighted, I get a smile on my face.

Scott Menzies (11)
Collydean Primary School, Glenrothes

Limerick

There was a young girl from Blackpool
Who would never get ready for school
She'd lay in her bed
Eating nothing but bread
She went to school looking like a fool.

Sean Ramage (8)
Collydean Primary School, Glenrothes

Glenrothes

G lorious Glenrothes
L ovely sights to see
E normous town park
N ice places to visit
R othes pit was flooded
O ur town in Scotland is the best
T he mines have all closed
H elp Glenrothes stay clean - recycle!
E veryone should see the hippos
S uper Glenrothes.

Amy Hall (8)
Collydean Primary School, Glenrothes

Sean Paul

S ean is the best
E veryone is
A big fan of him
N obody will say

P aul I don't like you
A ll fans
U nderstand the music, he
L ikes it.

Curtis Edwards (8)
Collydean Primary School, Glenrothes

2 Fast 2 Furious

B rian makes me laugh,
R acing lots of cars,
I really like him very much
A nd he is the greatest,
N ow he has got a brand new car.

Gary Dillon (8)
Collydean Primary School, Glenrothes

Idol Acrostic Poem

H arry waves his wand
A round and around
R eal good magic
R on is Harry's best, best friend
'Y ou're the best Harry,' everyone says

P eople wave magic about
O ver Hogwarts
T ap, tap on the ground
T ick-tock, tick-tock goes the clock at night
E veryone chewing on the dinner table
R ain tapping on the windows.

Chelsea Gourlay (8)
Collydean Primary School, Glenrothes

Winter

W inter is cold
I cicles are falling
N orth Pole is cold
T o be warm in the winter
E veryone likes the snow
R unning in the snow.

Daniel Whiteley (8)
Collydean Primary School, Glenrothes

Winter

W inter is a very cold time of year
I cicles are falling
N ests are getting built by robins
T oday it is snowing
E verybody is wearing gloves
R aking in the leaves.

Amy Walker (8)
Collydean Primary School, Glenrothes

When I Am . . .

When I am excited I can jump to the stars,
When I am sad I'm as low as the ground,
When I am happy I'm as bright as a light bulb,
When I am grumpy the whole world dies,
When I am jolly dolphins squeak high,
When I am frightened the flowers just fall,
When I am surprised I feel like a prize,
When I am moody I've got black eyes,
When I am angry the animals are all scared,
When I am delighted I'm over the moon.

John Chapman (11)
Collydean Primary School, Glenrothes

Emotions

When I am happy my face fills with glee,
When I am frightened it's not like I'm me
When I am angry I sort of grumble
When I am hungry my tummy rumbles
When I am moody I am such a grouch
When I am tired I fall asleep on the couch
When I am excited I jump up and down on my bed
When I am grumpy I say things that I shouldn't have said
When I am sad I feel small and weak
When I am happy I can ride my bike to the mountain peak!

Aimee Thomson (11)
Collydean Primary School, Glenrothes

A Lonely Frog

There once was a lonely dog
Who saw a lonely looking frog
They went in the park
And the lonely dog barked
And they both fell into the bog.

Jake Brown (8)
Collydean Primary School, Glenrothes

Winter Poem

The snaw is awfie cauld
Ma lugs are bright red
The snawball fight is starting
Na time ta sleep in bed

Got a massive snawball
No gonna waste it on you
Instead I'll build a snawman
Then fight till the day is through

Came back in the marning
Snaw is still here
Sat beside ma snawman
Ta me he's awfie dear

Went back in the marning
The snaw has turned ta ice
Tried ta find ma snawman
He was lost ta ma sicht.

Lindsey Gassner (11)
Collydean Primary School, Glenrothes

Fireworks

Light a rocket, up it goes
Faster and faster, when it stops no one knows
Then it stops and gives a roar
Everyone is quiet once more

The colours of the Catherine wheel
Green, red and blue like steel
Twisting, turning, beautiful, bright
All goes on during the night

Here comes another bang! Boom!
Roman candle up with a zoom!
Fireworks fast they just go pop!
All these colours never stop.

Emma Jex (11)
Collydean Primary School, Glenrothes

My Bedroom

My bedroom is very cluttered
It's also very messy
But that's because it's tiny
It's upstairs and it's violet
It's full of swirls
Inside only girls
In there is a telly
On a unit made of pine
Inside there will be books
No crooks
Nobody can see in
For a veil covers my window
There's a wardrobe full of clothes
You cannot see my pillow
For it's covered with stuffed toys
And my corner full of art
It's light
And just right
It's my bedroom.

Jasmine Stenhouse (10)
Collydean Primary School, Glenrothes

Spirits

Cold and murk
The spirits lurk
They creep into your window
At night they run away from light
But they never say so

      Spirits, spirits
      Scary spirits
      Hey, hey go away.

Scott McKeen (9)
Collydean Primary School, Glenrothes

People

People, people, people
People, people, people
They work
They discover
They pull over the cover
People, people, people.

They sleep
They weep
The farmers have sheep
People, people, people.

They go to school
They knit all kinds of wool
People, people, people.

They build
They are skilled
And they need to get filled
People!

Peter Woodbridge (9)
Collydean Primary School, Glenrothes

Numbers

Numbers, numbers waiting to be found
Numbers, numbers all around
Numbers, numbers in the dark
Numbers, numbers in the park
Numbers, numbers, numbers hide
Numbers, numbers, numbers outside
Numbers, numbers in the school
Numbers, numbers are so cool
Numbers!

Rachel Scott (10)
Collydean Primary School, Glenrothes

My Best Friend

My best friend is the greatest friend you could have
She is funny and acts silly
She tells me all her secrets and tells me all her jokes
Her hair is silky and blonde.

We play in the park with our dogs
At school we play with each other
We do everything together
When I go to my gran's, she comes too.

When we come home from my gran's we go on Rollerblades
On Mondays she comes over to my house and we go swimming.
On Tuesdays I go to her's, we go to McDonald's with her mum
On Wednesdays we go to swimming lessons.

On Thursdays we go to karate
On Fridays we go to baton twirling
On Saturdays we go to my gran's
And on Sundays we go to her gran's.

My best friend is Danielle Jorden.

Shannon Batchelor (9)
Collydean Primary School, Glenrothes,

Writing

Writing makes my hand sore
Just like it does anytime before.
Teacher's think writing's good,
But not when it makes you in a bad mood.

Oops I made a mistake.
Oh for goodness sake.
Why do I have to go to school,
Where all the teachers rule?

Writing, my hand slippy,
Then it makes my fingers nippy.
Drawing lines with rulers are OK
But writing sentences, no way!

Rachel Barnet (9)
Collydean Primary School, Glenrothes

Football

Standing there waiting for the whistle to blow
Against the hardest team in the league I suppose
The whistle blows
Everyone runs
They pass the ball.

My heart is pumping frantically, I run to tackle
Swoosh! I kicked the ball as hard as I could
The ball went flying like I just flung some food.

Running and running as fast as I could
They look so stunning in their big black boots
I looked so shrimpy to them
Huge men
At last we get the ball

Bang! The ball flies into the air
It goes in the net
I was jumping in the air saying loudly
'We won!'

John McArthur (9)
Collydean Primary School, Glenrothes

The Dragon

The dragon is hot
The dragon is cold
But when it is winter
It starts to get old

> The dragon breathes fire
> The dragon breathes ice
> But when he is hungry
> He just eats mice.

Barry Farmer (11)
Collydean Primary School, Glenrothes

Hidden Treasure

Hidden treasure
Hidden treasure
Where are you?

Hidden treasure
Hidden treasure
I will find you

Searching through the jungle in the scorching heat
Who could even try to dig in this tremendous heat.

Hidden treasure
Hidden treasure
Where are you?

Hidden treasure
Hidden treasure
I will find you

Searching through this water in and out
I go how could I try to dig in the tremendous heat.

Hidden treasure
Hidden treasure
Where are you?

Hidden treasure
Hidden treasure
I have found you.

Rebecca Wilson (10)
Collydean Primary School, Glenrothes

Clowns

I like clowns because they're funny
Their funny red noses and big feet
I like their tricks and their fuzzy wuzzy hair
And the different colours that they like to wear.

Gina Bishop (10)
Collydean Primary School, Glenrothes

Fast Cars

I love fast cars,
Impretzas and Sky lines,
Ferraris and Zondas,
The greatest cars of all time.

I know a guy with a Suburu,
It's shiny blue with gold alloys,
I love the sound of its turbo,
Full spec with all the toys.

One day I want a Zonda,
A black one with tinted glass,
With red neon lights,
But my test I still have to pass.

I like to collect fast cars,
Models and posters I like best,
So I keep dreaming of my own fast car,
Let's hope I pass my test.

Keith Rodger (11)
Collydean Primary School, Glenrothes

The Lion

The lion was happy
The lion was angry
The lion ate a man.

The lion was happy
The lion was angry
The lion ate the man
The lion was mad.

The lion was happy
The lion was angry
The lion ate the man
The lion was mad
The lion was happy again.

George Morrison (11)
Collydean Primary School, Glenrothes

Summer

Summer is the time
Summer is the way
So if you want me to pay
You're gonna have to say.

The sun is rising, the moon's away
I'm running through the dawn and it's time to pay
Sun is cool, sun is hot
I thought I was too hot.

Sometimes I'm hot, sometimes I'm cool
And so are you
The sun is rising and the moon's away
I'm running through the dawn and it's time to pay.

I thought I was fine, but I'm too hot
I like the sun, it's very hot.
So if you like the sun you're my friends too.

Kyle Harrower (10)
Collydean Primary School, Glenrothes

Harry Potter

H arry Potter is the best
A nything is possible
R unning well he finds things out
R aining or not he doesn't care
Y oung students at Hogwarts

P ots and potions are his type
O gres can catch a train, but they will feel his pain
T here's a terror everywhere he goes
T rolls may be big, but not as smart as Harry
E veryone should cheer
R elax, he wouldn't hurt you.

Stefanie Heron (8)
Collydean Primary School, Glenrothes

Cars

A Subaru is fast, it will not come last
You can run, you can have fun
But you can't make fun of a Subaru
Because it won't come last because it is fast
You will come last, because you are not fast.
You won't beat it
You will have to eat it
A Subaru is fast, it won't come last
You will come last
I am fast
You can come last if you are not fast
I won't come last
I am fast
If you come last you are not fast.
Lines are time of me
Winning the race
You are a pancake face
A Subaru is fast, it will not come last
Because it is fast you will come last
Because you are not fast, you will come last.

Sean Perrie (9)
Collydean Primary School, Glenrothes

Summer Kids

S plash! Swimming in the pools
U p in the trees the caterpillars eat
M any fruits grow on the trees
M elons yellow and juicy too
E ating and drinking is the best part
R abbit sunbathing in the sun.

K ids are excited about coming in the pools
I t's such a nice day so come along and play
D rinking juice is very cool
S ummer is the best thing today.

Hayley McKenna (8)
Collydean Primary School, Glenrothes

I'm At The Seaside

I'm at the seaside, I'm at the seaside
I can see a boat
I can see the rock pools
I can see sand, worms and stones
I can see a crab as well.

I'm at the seaside, I'm at the seaside
There are amusements at the top of the beach
There are lots of people round about
There are cars all over
The sun is out.

I'm at the seaside, I'm at the seaside
Nearly time to go walking up the beach
'Can we get an ice cream Mum?'
'No, no, no,'
'Why not? Why not? Why not?'
'All right, go on then,'
'Thanks Mum.'

I'm off from the seaside, I'm off from the seaside
And on the way home
Hey that was great fun.

I'm off from the seaside, I'm off from the seaside
Just going down the street
Just going in the drive
Going straight into the house, switching the TV on
Straight to children's programmes
Dad's home, Dad's home
'Hey Dad we had great fun at the seaside!'

I'm off from the seaside, I'm off from the seaside.

Sean Farrell (10)
Collydean Primary School, Glenrothes

The Seasons

Spring

In the spring animals are born
And all sorts of lovely flowers are growing.

Summer

Now comes summer.
Summer is very warm
Some people have barbecues
There is never a storm
People go everywhere in summer
It is great fun.

Autumn

And then we come to autumn
In autumn all the leaves fall off the trees
There are all sorts of colours on the leaves
Some are red, some are yellow, some are brown
Sometimes even gold
I like autumn
It is bright and beautiful.

Winter

Then last of all comes winter
In winter you can play in the snow
It's very cold you know
So you need to put warm clothes on
You can make snowmen and snow angels
I think winter is my favourite season of all.

Morgan Swan (10)
Collydean Primary School, Glenrothes

The Snowman And The Ice - Haiku

Building a snowman
The snowman slowly melting
I saw icicles.

Kenneth Morris (8)
Collydean Primary School, Glenrothes

Summer

Summer, summer, summer is here
It's time to give a really big cheer
Hip hip hooray, it's time to play
All the sand, sea and sun
It is all so fun.

Night is cool
Day is hot
You can get burnt, but really so what?
Go with a friend
And run end to end
This day has now come to an end.

It is time to go home now, you and your friend
You have had your fun
So has the sun
1, 2, 3
And that is me (finished).

Shannon Blaney (10)
Collydean Primary School, Glenrothes

Harry Potter

H arry Potter is the best
A nd everyone said he'll pass his test
R ain won't stop him, he's the one.
R on Weasley is his best friend
Y eah Harry

P ots and cauldrons, that's his game
O gres will feel the pain
T ogether with his friends he will be the best
T eamwork is what he does
E verybody better run
R un everyone.

Michael Currie (8)
Collydean Primary School, Glenrothes

The Beach

The sand is soft
The sea is cold
The sea is wavy
The sky is clear
There are shipwrecks in the sand
The sand is blowing at your legs
The stones are smooth
People are sunbathing
There is seaweed on the sand
There are rock pools people can look in
There are deck chairs on the soft sand
Little children are making sandcastles
There is sand on the bottom of your feet
The sun is shining
The shells are cracked
You can paddle in the sea
You can jump over the waves
Everybody is packing the car
Going all the way home
Nearly home in your car.

Steven Smith (9)
Collydean Primary School, Glenrothes

Glenrothes

G lorious Glenrothes
L ovely sights to see
E normous town park
N ice places to visit
R othes pit was flooded
O ur town in Scotland is the best
T he mines have all closed
H elp Glenrothes stay clean - recycle
E veryone should see the hippos
S uper Glenrothes.

Aletia Robertson (8)
Collydean Primary School, Glenrothes

The Beach

The sun is shining
The waves are still
The sand is blowing
The shells are shiny
The stones are smooth.

Everybody is there having picnics
Playing around
Swimming in the sea
Making sandcastles
1, 2, 3

Now it's time to go
Everybody is packing
Now it's empty
The sun is setting behind the sea.

Now's it's morning, it's full again
The sun is gone
The waves are rushing
The boats are going over humps
Everybody is running away.

The streets are flooded
No one is out
They're all watching TV
Some are still sleeping
1, 2, 3

Everyone is back at the beach
Swimming,
Playing games
Resting
Making sandcastles
Having picnics to 1, 2, 3.

Nicola Forsyth (9)
Collydean Primary School, Glenrothes

Going To Space

Going to space
Going to space
Oh, it must be ace
We could have a race
Right through space.

Going to space
Going to space
Get a chase
We could make a base
We could trace different base.

Going to space
Going to space
A peeking face
As we run through space
I've packed my case
Let's go up to space.

Going to space
Going to space
I can't find a trace
At the alien base
Now I tied my lace
Let's go up to space.

Going to space
Going to space
Now I have found
My secret place
Let's go up to space.

Nicola Gallacher (10)
Collydean Primary School, Glenrothes

Dogs

Dogs are friendly
Dogs are kind
Dogs are playful
Dogs are man's best friend

Dogs are guard dogs
Dogs are intelligent
Dogs are cuddly
Dogs are man's best friend

Dogs are strong
Dogs are gentle
Dogs are funny
Dogs are man's best friend

Dogs are bold
Dogs are cool
Dogs are fluffy
Dogs are man's best friend

Dogs are cute
Dogs are loud
Dogs are silly
Dogs can do tricks
Dogs are man's best friend.

Hannah Blackwood (9)
Collydean Primary School, Glenrothes

Autumn

A utumn is in the air
U nder the tree it is warm
T rees are waving in the breeze
U mbrellas are blowing about
M ist in the mountains
N ow it is autumn!

Callum Penman (8)
Collydean Primary School, Glenrothes, Glenrothes

Love And Hate

I love chocolate because it's nice and delicious especially Galaxy!
I hate spiders they make me shiver
I love cartoons because they are cool and funny
I hate fish because it is slimy and ucky
I love myself because I am nice
I hate healthy food it is rotten
I love cats they are nice, soft and furry
I hate Lord of the Rings, it is rubbish
I love Harry Potter, it is super duper cool
I hate writing it doesn't suit me
I love school, well most of the time
I hate getting out of bed early for school
I love junk food like crisps and sweets
I hate doing my homework
I love it when it's the weekend
I hate getting shouted at
I love being naughty to my mum and dad
I hate it when my dad watches football
I love it when I get Chinese and McDonald's
I hate wearing dresses
I love being just me!

Phillipa Drummond (10)
Collydean Primary School, Glenrothes

Stormy Night

S tormy night
T ime to hide under beds
O r on the sofa
R un, run very fast
M y, my it's finally over
Y eah, let's celebrate.

Kane Easson (10)
Collydean Primary School, Glenrothes

Cartoons

C artoons are stupid and silly
A t the start it sometimes has flashbacks
R aphael is my favourite character in Teenage Mutant Ninja Turtles
T hey are terribly funny
O ver and over I watch them
O zzy and Drix is a funny cartoon.
N icktoons TV has good shows on it
S pider-Man is very boring.

Corey Carnegie (9)
Collydean Primary School, Glenrothes

Fishing

There was a young fellow named Gary
Who liked to go fishing with Barry
He borrowed a rod
To the barn he did plod
His other friend was Harry.

Hannah Pollock (8)
Collydean Primary School, Glenrothes

My Room

My room
Is full of stuff
Also it is a mess
Can't be bothered to tidy up
That's me.

Craig Ross (10)
Collydean Primary School, Glenrothes

Keith And His Teeth

There was an old man called Keith
He liked to play with his teeth
He's like a stick
But he's as hard as a brick
And he likes to eat lots of beef.

Scott Blackwood (11)
Collydean Primary School, Glenrothes

Waterfall - Haiku

Water racing down
Bubbles floating all around
Bubbles popping, pop.

Chelsie Courts (10)
Collydean Primary School, Glenrothes

Rain

Dripping from leaves,
Dropping on to the roof,
Clattering on the slates.
The road is flooding.
Water is pouring
From the river.
The drain is flooding.
Water is hissing in the pipes
Rain is dribbling off the plants
Splashing on to the pavement
Plopping into the puddles.

Corin Arkieson (7)
Cranshaws Primary School, Duns

Oh Chocolate, Chocolate

Chocolate, chocolate
You're wonderful stuff
I love you chocolate
I can't get enough
You're covered with magic
And you're sprinkled with mint
Chocolate, chocolate
Give me some more please.

Chocolate, chocolate
You're very tasty
You're hard and soft
You're sweet around
There's slurpy chocolate
All over my plate
Chocolate, chocolate
I think of you so much every day
I think you are great
Chocolate, chocolate
I love you a lot
You're flaky, you're creamy
Delicious and cold
Gobble you down
I can't get enough
Chocolate, chocolate
You're wonderful stuff
The flavour is good.

Jodie Nardone (10)
Crossgates Primary School, Cowdenbeath

Travel

I like to travel by
Bus and by car
There are lots of other ways to travel
But these two are quick.

I like to travel by
Boat and by ship
There are other ways to travel
But these two are nice.

I like to travel by
Hot air balloon and by plane
There are other ways to travel
But these two are fun.

There are good ways to travel
But my best is a broomstick
I have not rode one yet
But I'm going to soon.

Alyssa Lax (9)
Crossgates Primary School, Cowdenbeath

There Are Many Ways To Travel

There are many ways to travel
The one I like is my motorbike
It's faster than a jet
Which I go on at every chance
I ride on my motorbike and that is what I like
It's better than a normal bike
Because it's my motorbike.

Ross Shepherd (9)
Crossgates Primary School, Cowdenbeath

The Quarrel

I quarrelled with my sister
I know what it's about
It's about that silly laptop
She really made me shout
It started off alright
But ended up a fight
She really loves to play on it
And I just love to write.

She knew that I was busy
Of course that's why she did it
She started to be stupid
She was acting like a baby
Not like a grown-up kid,
She was in the bad books
And I was in the good books
Then my mum came in and said
'You two better stop *now!*'

Sarah Turner (9)
Crossgates Primary School, Cowdenbeath

The Way I Like To Travel

I travel on a bus,
It's very, very slow,
But when I drive a sports car
I like to burn the tar.

I travel on a train
It goes zoom, zoom, zoom.
When I ride a bike
I'm really just a tyke.

I travel on a glider
It's powered by the air
I want to fly a rocket
And I want to be famous like
    Neil Armstrong

Jake Simpson (9)
Crossgates Primary School, Cowdenbeath

Jet Tastic!

I will travel in a jet plane
Travel everywhere
I will fly right up high
And soar without a care.

Zoom over the countries
Right across the earth
Whizzing through the universe
I'm going to land at Perth.

Loop-de-loop
Up and down
Fast and slow
Round and round.

I will travel in a jet plane
Travel everywhere
Flying right up high
Soar without a care.

Emma Park (9)
Crossgates Primary School, Cowdenbeath

The Way I Like To Travel

I like to travel in style
For many miles
In a lovely limousine

I like to travel in the air
When the wind's in my hair
In a hot air balloon.

I like to travel fast
With the EastEnder's cast
In a zooming car.

I like to travel in water
Though I could be hotter
In a yellow yacht.

Chloe Meiklem (9)
Crossgates Primary School, Cowdenbeath

Travel

There are many ways to travel
There are many ways to ride
You can trot
And you can canter
You can jump and gallop too.

I can travel by a rocket
With a dragon in my pocket
I hurtle into space
With my dragon there too.

But the nicest way to travel
Is to zoom in a plane
Into the white clouds above
And fly like a dove.

Imogen Brindle (10)
Crossgates Primary School, Cowdenbeath

Travel

There are many ways to travel
But the one I like is . . .
Speeding on my bike
But I always wanted to go up into space
And zoom in a rocket,
With a sweet in my pocket
Or maybe gallop on a horse
And force the horse to go.
There are many ways to travel
I would like to travel through the air
On a super duper jet
And you can bet
It's fast
And it won't last.

Lindsay McGouldrick (9)
Crossgates Primary School, Cowdenbeath

Many Ways To Fly

There are many ways to fly
I like to fly in a jet
I go very high and almost touch the sky
And when I come back down, I'm very, very shy.

There are many ways to fly
High up in the air
Sometimes I cry
Or maybe it's not fair.

There are many ways to fly
Sometimes I am sick
Maybe I get an itch
Or somebody decides to play a trick.

There are many ways to fly
I like to fly in style
Sometimes for a mile
But the best way of all is flying in a jet.

Ben Polhill (9)
Crossgates Primary School, Cowdenbeath

Pizza! Pizza!

Pizza! Pizza!
I love you
You taste cheesy
You crumble in my mouth
You bubble up like a monster
My mum gives you to me so much
I'm mad for you
So give me some, oh please
My mum asks, 'Do you want pepperoni?'
I say *'No!'*

Carly Miller (9)
Crossgates Primary School, Cowdenbeath

Chocolate, O Chocolate

I love you the most
You're hard and minty
Chocolate, o chocolate
It's greasy, it's small
It comes in large bars, milk, white or dark
I love it the most
Chocolate, o chocolate
You're wonderful stuff
I could get a whole box
I just can't get enough
I love the chocolate it's hard
I have to get a sharp knife
Chocolate, o chocolate you're magic
I love you the most when
The bubbles tickle in my mouth.

Claire Cuthill (9)
Crossgates Primary School, Cowdenbeath

How To Travel

If you travel in a train
You must be a pain
If you travel in a rocket
You must remember to travel
With a penny in your pocket
If you travel in a jet
You must remember to bring your pet
Remember to zoom, zoom in a Ferrari
And skid on a mud track with a Subaru.

Sam Penman (9)
Crossgates Primary School, Cowdenbeath

Chocolate! Chocolate!

Chocolate! Chocolate!
You're magical stuff
I love you chocolate
I can't get enough
You're sweet and explosive
You're sprinkled in mint
Oh, give me some more please!

Chocolate! Chocolate!
Piled in a mound
You're flaky and chewy
You're really hard
You explode in my mouth
You're all in my mouth.

Kara Westwood (9)
Crossgates Primary School, Cowdenbeath

Pizza, Pizza

Pizza, pizza
When my mum makes you
I say, 'Yes.'
Pizza, pizza
I love you so much
Pizza, pizza
You're covered in cheese
Pizza, pizza
You're covered in cheese sauce
Oh, pizza your base so sweet
Pizza, pizza
Your base round the edge is crispy
Pizza, pizza
You're delicious Italian food.

Steven Murphy (9)
Crossgates Primary School, Cowdenbeath

Edinburgh Trip

Edinburgh trip, Edinburgh trip off we go
On our Edinburgh trip.

On the bus we go chugging along, chugging along,
On the bus we go.

At the hotel, hotter than ever
At the hotel.

In the rooms, in the rooms watching out the window,
In the rooms.

Going out to bowling, going out to bowling,
David gets a strike, going out to bowling!

All things done, all things done, waiting for the bus,
All things done!

Edinburgh trip, Edinburgh trip all sad and quiet
After our Edinburgh trip.

Shaun Mitchell (11)
Cullen Primary School, Buckie

Animals

As fast as a cheetah, as slow as a snail,
A tiny little mouse, a great white whale.

As bright as a parrot, as brown as a bear,
A stripy zebra, a bouncy hare.

As cheeky as a monkey, as boring as a cat,
A playful puppy, an ugly rat.

As dead as a dodo, as slimy as a frog,
That's all the animals, wait we forgot the dog!

Liam Donn (11)
Cullen Primary School, Buckie

Mary Kings Close

Long ago in Mary Kings Close
Lived hundreds of people, maybe even a ghost.
Up and down the close people walked
And the ghosts like their victims to be stalked
Down in Annie's room, Annie will cry
While the doctor's son is about to die.

All of this because of the 'black death'
That the rats carried to lay people to rest.
In the close 'Guardi loo' is heard
The waste lands on the biggest nerd!
The close is a very creepy place,
Up and down the children liked to race.

Now I've told you about Mary Kings Close
You should visit it some day and I hope you don't meet a ghost!

Christopher Gray (11)
Cullen Primary School, Buckie

On The Farm

Broom, broom, broom over the hills and far away
Farmer Dan gets up each and every day
To feed his animals far and wide,
Throughout the countryside.

Cows, pigs and sheep
Weep for their grain or meat.

Hens, chickens, ducks and geese
Quiver for their pecking feast.

Horses gallop along the stream
As farmer Dan goes home for his tea!

Suzanne Grant (12)
Cullen Primary School, Buckie

Laser Quest

Laser Quest is brilliant!
It's really, really great.
My fighter name is Monster,
It was real, good mate.

Mind the person in the cloak
Gave us a right good scare.
Made me jump out of my skin,
It really wasn't fair.

Remember Mrs Calder?
She was a sight to be feared the most.
Coz when in the ultra violet
She was glowing like a ghost!

Edinburgh was brilliant!
Can't believe it was so good,
And if Mrs Calder and Mrs Stewart weren't there,
I'd be in a terrible mood!

Chloe McCluskey (11)
Cullen Primary School, Buckie

Waiting For My Friend

Alone I stand waiting
Waiting for someone.
I look around waiting
Waiting for my friend.

The cold air blows through my hair.
My lips chapped, my face white
Waiting for my friend.

Alone, the trees start blowing
And the car lights glowing.
My friend arrives.

Morven Robb (12)
Cullen Primary School, Buckie

Outside

Outside the black ebony sky
A sparkling diamond hanging in the darkness
Stars bordering the diamond
Like some sort of picture.

Outside, strange quiet sounds
Dogs howling in the moonlight
Cats creeping silently over silver ground
Like hissing strange sounds.

Outside branches swaying
The wind hitting against them
Whispering creepy, soft noises
Like someone whispering something in my ear.

Outside, shadows weird and slowly passing
Cats, dogs, people, children
Running and jumping about
Like a dog chasing a cat.

Amber Cox (11)
Cullen Primary School, Buckie

The Titanic

At the night I tried to sleep
I think back now and I start to weep
I close my eyes and the thoughts rush to my head
All the people that now are dead.

That tragic night I tried to forget
Then I think of the people I met
They were so nice, they didn't deserve to die
But now I think I can't even say goodbye.

Ben Addison (12)
Cullen Primary School, Buckie

Me And The Sea

Every time I look at the sea
I turn around and jump with glee
On the beach is where I want to be
Except when my mum calls me in for tea.

In the summer I like to jump off the pier
I'm so glad it's so very near
It doesn't cost much, it's not very dear
It's healthier than drinking lots of beer!

In the autumn I like to paddle
I spend time with horses, sitting on a saddle
I enter competitions in the hope of a medal
I also ride my bike, I like to pedal.

In the winter the sea is cold
Don't jump off the pier I am often told
The winter sun looks like gold
But the dark nights have got a hold

In the spring everything is starting to grow
The sea is warming up, but it is very slow
The gardeners are starting to mow
And often that is when the tide is low.

That's my year about the sea
I hope it has told you a bit about me
The things I do, where I like to be
You see in Cullen I am allowed to be free.

Grace Joyce (11)
Cullen Primary School, Buckie

Alone

Silence. A cold chill.
The sea is the jaws of a hungry wolf
Waiting to engulf me.
I walk along the powdery sand,
Alone.

Stillness. Shadows dance and leap.
The moon is a giant suspended pearl.
An expert in stealth
One long shadow walks,
Alone.

Silver. Star of night.
Guides the crested majestic wings of the sea.
Long arms of silence engulf,
Me.
Alone.

Lydia Francis (11)
Cullen Primary School, Buckie

Fire Dance

F lames spring into
I ndigo skies
R aging at the
E choing winds.

D arkness falls
A nd fire weakens
N ow flames fade
C ease
E verything is quiet, as the fire dies.

Sasha Reid (11)
Cullen Primary School, Buckie

A Visit To The Zoo

Cheetahs roaring in their cage
Rhinos storming about in a rage
Giraffes' heads nearly touching the sky
Their necks about a mile high
The day we went for a visit to the zoo.

Monkeys eating lots of bananas
Let's go and see the spitting llamas
Where are the bears? They're nowhere to be seen
There's Mrs Stewart, I wonder where she has been
The day we went for a visit to the zoo.

The seals clap their flippers and eat lots of fish
They take it from your hands, not from a dish
Their skin is so shiny, silky and wet
I'm going to ask my mum if I can get one for a pet!
The day we went for a visit to the zoo.

In the reptile house, Grace, Tamsin and me
Because we're so small we can hardly see!
But Amber and Melissa, what have they got?
They've got a snake and it eats a lot!
The day we went for a visit to the zoo.

The zebras are at the top of a hill
And the lions are looking for something to kill
It's time for the penguin parade and they look so funny
The tigers look fierce, but they're hot because it is sunny
The day we went for a visit to the zoo.

It's time to go home, the bus is here
We all go to the shop, but everything is so dear
There's someone missing, oh no, I think it's Ben
Mrs Clader shouts, '*Stop!* I think he's in the lion's den!'
The day we went for a visit to the zoo.

Chloe McGregor (12)
Cullen Primary School, Buckie

I Remember

I remember, I remember
When I was a little boy
One day my big brother stole my favourite toy,
He made me laugh, he made my cry,
He even told my mum a lie!
He said he hadn't got the toy
That rightfully belonged to her youngest boy.

I remember, I remember
The great big roar
He let out when his bottom was sore!
He got a smack and then said he was sorry
So I gave him back my favourite lorry.
After all he is my brother
And in the toy box, I've got another.

David Allan (12)
Cullen Primary School, Buckie

At The Circus

A t the circus the noise is loud,
T he on and off cheering of the crowd!

T ricks from the elephants, jokes from clowns
H igh rope walking, magicians in gowns.
E veryone smiles and stares with glee.

C annonballs and juggling for all to see,
I nside or out it makes no odds.
R eal smiles as the crowd applauds,
C ircus time here is almost done.
U ncertain or not if it was great fun
S oon the noise will all be gone,
   Silence as night-time comes!

Melissa Mair (11)
Cullen Primary School, Buckie

A Night View

The night is quiet.
Silence kills everything.
Only the lone owl makes a weary noise.
Silence, calms, everything.

The moon is silver.
A silver pearl travelling through a dark sky.
Switching on and off as it floats behind clouds.
Brightness, lights, night.

The night is still.
Stillness calms all.
No loud noise dare be made.
Movement, is, stopped.

James Morrison (11)
Cullen Primary School, Buckie

Silent Night

Silently sleeps the forest
The snow lies like a glimmering
White sheet of shimmering pearls.
Icy features lurk.

Night. Darkness unfolds
Only the pearly moon gives light
Guiding the shadows.
Everything is white.

Silently flows the river
Peaceful and quiet,
The moon descends
As the dawn rises.

Judith Mair (11)
Cullen Primary School, Buckie

Mrs Calder And Her Class

Away in a village called Cullen
There is a school, which Mrs Hendry is running
In this school, there is a Class 7
And Mrs Calder is the teacher from Heaven
She has a really barking mad class
And they all really hate doing maths.
In there, there is Christopher Gray and Emma Hay,
David Allan is in there too,
With Lydia, Sasha and Judith who
Is best friends with Stephanie Strachan
Who likes Chloe 2 who is totally quackin'
Where as Chloe 1 is really fun,
Who likes Melissa, who loves to run
Tamsin sits opposite her
Suzanne would love some leopard fur
Amber and Morven are really cool,
While Colin and Geordie will always be fools.
Grace does not really like James
And Liam watches 'Still Game'
Shaun loves drawing things
And when Mrs Calder shouts, Zenc's eardrums ring.
Ben and Timothy sit at the same table
And Ryan has an aunty Mabel.
So now you've been introduced to my class
I hope you give us and my poem a definite pass!

Emma Hay (12)
Cullen Primary School, Buckie

Tigers

Tigers with their mysterious stripes,
Kill their prey with just a few swipes.
With flashing green eyes,
They look to the skies,
And make their way home.

Katrina Hay (11)
Eccles/Leitholm Primary School, Kelso

My Pony

Ears flat against your hairy head,
As you rise from your warm straw bed.
Broad, strong back,
Patience is what you lack.
When I put your saddle on, you rear up high,
Then in the field, you throw me in the sky.
Yet even though you're very bad,
I'm glad,
That I've got you as my pony!
Naughty Boston
Bad Boston
Hairy Boston
Cheeky Boston
Fat Boston
Slobbery Boston
Lazy Boston
Boston you are all these things
You are the best pony in the world!

Jade Hebdon (11)
Eccles/Leitholm Primary School, Kelso

Star My Little Dog

I have a black Labrador
That I couldn't love more.
She's short and stubby
And rather tubby.
She carries sticks
And give me licks.
She's quite smelly
With her big belly.
I wouldn't swap her for the world
You are my little star.

Charlie Davis (10)
Eccles/Leitholm Primary School, Kelso

The Foal

I remember when you were one hour old,
I brought you into the stable so you would not get cold.
You tried to stand up like your mother,
But she put straw on you as a cover.
Everyone said 'That's a stunning foal,
Your mare sure has scored a fine goal!'
In the end I decide to call you Kendal,
Because you were so cute and gentle.
Now you do shows, because you're all grown up,
You are such a brilliant jumper you won the cup!
Kendal you are my dream come true,
I love you pony, I really do!

Hope Brown (11)
Eccles/Leitholm Primary School, Kelso

Animals

Rabbits, rabbits they're so fast
Cute and very fluffy
Cheetahs, cheetahs are the fastest animals in the world
They're spotty and you can never spot one
Lions, lions they're the kings of the jungle
They're fluffy, but very, very fierce
Giraffes, giraffes they're very skinny
They have a long neck and a spotty body
Sabre tooth's, sabre tooth's they're extinct
They're scary and have very big teeth
Lots of animals.

Shekira James (8)
Kenmore Primary School, Kenmore by Aberfeldy

What To Do?

What to do with my little brother?
He's horrible and rude
He never eats his vegetables
And he's always in a mood
What to do with my little brother?
He never chews his food
What to do? He's never ever good
He's always being spoilt
And it's really not fair
And he's always being annoying
Cos he still pulls my hair
Whenever he's noisy
I put earmuffs on
And when it stops
The neighbours will come.

Chloe Bennett (9)
Kenmore Primary School, Kenmore by Aberfeldy

Happiness!

Lying on a tropical beach
Sipping fresh coconut milk
Spotting dark blue dolphins
Dancing through the waves
The sunset is red
Reflecting on the sparkling warm water.

Lying on a golden beach
At the end of a long hot day
I can faintly hear the
Palm trees swaying
In the evening breeze
I can still remember the feel
Splashing on my sun warmed skin.

Rosie Harrison Flower (9)
Kenmore Primary School, Kenmore by Aberfeldy

Food

Soft food
Hard food
Spicy food
All types
Of food.

Soft food
Is breakfast.

Hard food
Is lunch.

Spicy food is
Tea and lots
More

Soft food berries
Hard food apples
Spicy food curry and
Can you believe it?
There's lots more.

Munro Fraser (8)
Kenmore Primary School, Kenmore by Aberfeldy

Big Bad Bully

There is a big bad bully at my school
He is big, fat and ugly
When he is around there is always trouble
He is always in a gang or a small group
But really he is not that tough
Because all he is
Is a big fat bully!

Bradley Baird (10)
Kenmore Primary School, Kenmore by Aberfeldy

Animals

Hares are furry, hares are quite tall,
But compared to us, they're actually quite small.
Dolphins are rubbery and they like to dive,
But I wouldn't go too close to a beehive
Tigers are striped, they may look cute,
But don't get too close, or you will be the size of a newt.

Rosie Jo Thomas (8)
Kenmore Primary School, Kenmore by Aberfeldy

Winds

Very strong winds
Very strong winds
All types of winds
Soft winds, slow winds
Loud winds, quiet winds
Cold winds, warm winds

Robbie Olivier (9)
Kenmore Primary School, Kenmore by Aberfeldy

Off To The Shops

We're off to the shops
And there's lots we can buy.
We can buy:
Pick and mix and
Pens and
Milk and
Eggs and
Shoes and
A teddy bear and
Food and
Toys and
Books and
A swimming costume.

Isobel Murray John (7)
Muck Primary School, Mallaig

We're Off To The Shops

We're off to the shops and
There's lots to buy, we can buy:
Fake earrings and
New clothes and
Swimming things and
A horse and
Sweeties and
Jewellery and
A lock for my door and
Chocolate and
A swimming pool and
Stickers and
CDs and
A makeover kit and
Two lambs and
Pasta and
A cooker and
A chocolate orange and
Coke and
Drinks and
Some chocolate for Mummy and
Fishing stuff for Daddy.

Amy McFadzean (9)
Muck Primary School, Mallaig

Cheetah - Haiku

Cheetah, like the wind
Gaining quickly on its prey
Chasing a gazelle.

Jamie MacEwen (8)
Muck Primary School, Mallaig

Cats

Some cats are fat and like to lay on mats
Others are slim and like catching rats.

Some are lazy,
Some are crazy,

Some are happy,
Some are sad,
Some are calm,
Some are mad,

Some are white with stripes,
Some like playing with wipes,

Others are old and helpless,

But one thing they all have in common, they're all cute.

Eilidh MacKenzie (11)
Newhall Primary School, Dingwall

The Last Wild Horse

Hear hoofs on the sand of the last wild horse
In the land.

He owns the meadows and the woodland paths,
The last wild horse, the very last.

See him jump waves and streams,
Only a horse you see in dreams.

See the breeze on his mane
As he runs the open plain.

No one could tame him or take him in hand,
The strong wild stallion, the last in the land.

Victoria Hammond (10)
Newhall Primary School, Dingwall

The Ride

I went on a ride
With my friend by my side
Through all the dirt of the countryside
We rode in the wood
And then stopped for food
We did some downhill
Straight past a windmill
I fell in a trough
Which gave me a cough
My friend gave a laugh
Then just missed a calf
The hills were not small
And were no fun at all
All of a sudden
It happened in a flash
Upside down in a ditch
Looks like I had a *crash!*

Ryan Gault (11)
Newhall Primary School, Dingwall

At Work With Dad

Here we sit by a burn
Watching giant windmills turn,
Lorries come, lorries go
Some go fast, some go slow
They carry tonnes of stone you know
Diggers take out lots of peat
To make a road nice and neat
Lorries carry tonnes of rock
One more windmill from the dock
Over us the windmill's tower
Making more of Highland's power.

Catriona MacEachran (11)
Newhall Primary School, Dingwall

My Day At Contin

I raced down the downhill
I pushed up the uphill
I smashed into a tree
While my dad had a cup of tea
My sister was there,
But I didn't really care
I landed a drop
And got a big shock
We got to the car
Without a scar
We went to the chippy
And saw a hippy
When we got home
I had some honeycomb.

Stewart Thompson (11)
Newhall Primary School, Dingwall

The Beautiful Game

Football is great fun,
It really makes you run
And if you practise skills
You get more thrills
And your team cheers you on.

Beckham scores with magnificent free kicks,
Ronaldinho makes up lots of tricks
Perhaps one day you'll do the same
As practise is the price of fame,
Maybe World Cup here you come.

Michael Manson (11)
Newhall Primary School, Dingwall

All Alone

All alone I stand in a corner, all alone,
I sit by myself watching the clouds go by,
All alone I think I should become a loner.
I have no friends,
But if I did I'd be very happy,
But that is just a dream
So I just sit by myself
All alone.

Bronwen MacKenzie (10)
Newhall Primary School, Dingwall

Green Is . . .

A leaf drifting down,
And a tiny emerald in the Queen's crown.

An apple hanging on a tree,
And a strand of seaweed in the sea.

A juicy pear,
And soft grass growing everywhere.

A frog sitting by the pond,
And a bunch of grapes, of which I'm fond.

A cat's eye flashing in the dark,
And a tiny clump of moss on a tree's bark.

Heather Andrews (10)
New Pitsligo & St Johns Primary School, Fraserburgh

White Is . . .

All the clouds floating in the sky,
And the seagulls in a flock, flying by.

A polar bear at the North Pole,
And a small football being kicked into the goal.

A necklace of pearls round a lady's neck,
And the iceberg causing the Titanic shipwreck.

Part of my eye so that I can see you all,
And a telephone cable so that I can make a call.

A snowdrop, which brightens up the town,
And a graceful snowflake drifting slowly down.

Lynn Rennie (10)
New Pitsligo & St Johns Primary School, Fraserburgh

Red Is . . .

A clown's big nose,
And a garden rose.

A juicy raspberry,
And a ripe shiny cherry.

A fox's small paw,
And a lobster's sharp claw.

The colour of a flame,
And my cheeks when I get the blame.

My heart in my chest,
And an apple I like best!

Nicola Russell (11)
New Pitsligo & St Johns Primary School, Fraserburgh

Slimy, Slithering Sssnake

Slimy, slithering snake.
What will it make? What will it make?
A pancake, a birthday cake or a wedding cake?
Just what will you make? Just what will you make?
Mr green slimy, slithering snake!

Slimy, slithering snake.
What will it take? What will it take?
A milkshake, a rake, a sweet chocolate flake?
Just what will you take? Just what will you take?
Mr green slimy, slithering snake.

Slimy, slithering snake.
What will it break? What will it break?
The garden rake, the bridge over the lake?
Just what will you break? Just what will you break?
Mr green, slimy, slithering snake.

Oliver East (10)
New Pitsligo & St Johns Primary School, Fraserburgh

Green Is . . .

An emerald shining bright
And a lime coloured kite.

A lizard sitting in the sun
And lots of grasshoppers having fun.

A turtle swimming in the sea
And an apple eaten by a chimpanzee.

The cabbage on my dinner plate
And the tortoise who is always late.

Stephanie Logan (10)
New Pitsligo & St Johns Primary School, Fraserburgh

Claire The Bear

Claire the bear, who'll never share,
Who'll never share,
And if she does, it's very rare!
All she does is sit in her lair,
Unaware of anything there.

Claire the bear, who'll never share,
Just sits and stares,
Out of her lair.
All she does is sit in her lair,
Unaware of anything there.

Claire the bear, who'll never share,
Dyed her hair to give everyone a scare,
Claire the bear, gave everyone a scare,
Then went home to sit, in her lair,
Unaware of anything there.

Bryan Addison (10)
New Pitsligo & St Johns Primary School, Fraserburgh

Counting Rhyme

One boy having fun
Two blue shiny shoes
Three fat buzzy bees
Four grassy mowers.

Five wasps in a hive
Six bags of pick-n-mix
Seven dogs go to Heaven
Eight minutes late!

Nine glasses of fine wine
Ten men alive again
Eleven men playing sevens
Twelve big shelves.

Robert Morrow (9)
New Pitsligo & St Johns Primary School, Fraserburgh

If . . .

If my grandma was a bird
She would be a little robin,
With sparkling eyes that shimmered
In the red-hot sun.

If my grandma was a tree
She would be a beech tree
At the back of the garden
With birds that sing alluring songs.

If my grandma was a flower
She would be a tulip,
With her elegance and
Her soothing words of wisdom.

If my grandma was a child
She would keep her thoughts to herself,
And keep her secrets hidden
Like a quiet little mouse.

Hazel Duncan (11)
New Pitsligo & St Johns Primary School, Fraserburgh

War And Peace

The pain of war and misery,
That's what I have to look out of my window to see.
Men are dying,
People are crying
Men are dropping like leaves off a tree.

The pain and misery soon far away,
Children out playing in their backyards.
The memories they have,
Rotten and never to be forgotten.

Gary Robertson (11)
New Pitsligo & St Johns Primary School, Fraserburgh

If . . .

If my brother was a fairy tale
Character, he would be a giant,
A gigantic immoveable person.

If my brother was an animal
He would be a hare,
Uncatchable, rushing away like the wind.

If my brother was a famous person
He would be Jonny Wilkinson,
An energetic hero.

If my brother was an animal
He would be a dog,
Rough and playful
Hurting me every time.

Daniel Merritt (11)
New Pitsligo & St Johns Primary School, Fraserburgh

If . . .

If my sister was an animal
She'd be a hedgehog
Curling up into a little ball, sleeping.

If my sister was a fairytale creature
She'd be Snow White, always looking
To see if she looks good enough to go to a party.

If my sister was a popstar
She'd be Anastacia
Singing all the time,
Loudly.

If my sister was a country
She'd be Greece, everything going
Slowly and running behind schedule.

Frazer Hall (11)
New Pitsligo & St Johns Primary School, Fraserburgh

Who Am I?

To my mum I am someone to be proud of
To help her with the housework
And do anything for her if she is ill
And if I tidy my bedroom, she doesn't have to.

To my dad I am someone to playfight with
And watch the football with
I always make him cups of tea
And he picks me up from Guides.

My sister thinks I am kind and caring
She always plays football with me
She has a great sense of humour
We share everything together.

Rosie loves me lots and lots
She barks at me to take her for walks
I play with her in the garden
And train her to sit for food.

Holly Meall (11)
New Pitsligo & St Johns Primary School, Fraserburgh

War

The agony of war.
A shell, quick, duck!
Planes roaring, Bismarck boxing,
Soldiers screaming
Bombs exploding.
Fire ripping through towns,
Houses falling like a drunken man.
Murder, explosion, blood.

Steven Smith (11)
New Pitsligo & St Johns Primary School, Fraserburgh

If . . .

If my big, little brother was a footballer
He'd be the one that always scores
Quick at acting and fast at moving
Like a pair of motorbike wheels.

If my big, little brother was a movie star
He'd be the worst one alive
He wouldn't have a clue what to do
Like a thick banana.

If my big, little brother was a bee
He'd be the fastest one alive
Buzzing around all day and making noises
Like a 12 wheeled lorry.

If my big, little brother was a monkey
He'd be the quietest one on earth
He'd hardly ever make a sound
Like a pussycat.

Tanya Coe (11)
New Pitsligo & St Johns Primary School, Fraserburgh

War

Fighting snipers
Tattered and torn camouflage uniform,
Blood all over it
Livid face, in the forest where he's safe.
Guns banging, soldiers shouting,
Petrol bombs dropping next to him
Filling the forest
The fire roaring like a lion
Bang! Boom! Bang!

Michael Thomson (11)
New Pitsligo & St Johns Primary School, Fraserburgh

Nicky The Snake

Nicky the snake
Baked a cake
To take to the lake
With a milkshake.

Nicky the snake
Got a tummy ache
Then made a pancake
To eat at the lake
With her cake and milkshake.

Nicky the snake
Had a cake
When she had to take a break
On her way to the lake
With her cake and milkshake.

Sacha Callaghan   (10)
New Pitsligo & St Johns Primary School, Fraserburgh

Vickie The Snake

Vickie the snake
Baked a cake
And then on top, she put a flake.

Vickie the snake
She iced the cake
So that it would not break.

Vickie the snake
Drank with her cake
A thick and creamy strawberry milkshake.

Vickie the snake
Ate the whole cake
And then she had tummy ache.

Katy Coe   (9)
New Pitsligo & St Johns Primary School, Fraserburgh

The Grumpy Grizzly Bear

There once was a grumpy grizzly bear
Because he had no frizzy hair.
He had no frizzy hair,
Because he got a great big scare,
That silly, grumpy grizzly bear.

There once was a grumpy grizzly bear,
Who went for a walk with his chair,
While he was out, he met the mayor,
That silly, grumpy grizzly bear.

There once was a grumpy grizzly bear
Who really, really liked a pear.
And if you tried to take it, he would glare!
That silly, grumpy grizzly bear.

Rebecca McKean (11)
New Pitsligo & St Johns Primary School, Fraserburgh

Peace

Dancing, hearing
Singing, cheering
The laughter, the joking
Praising love and friendship
The smell of love and joy!
The singing, like music from an angel's voice.

Amy Howard (11)
New Pitsligo & St Johns Primary School, Fraserburgh

Peace

Evacuees arriving home,
Shouting to their mums,
Tears of joy, tears of sorrow
Wishing they'll survive tomorrow,
Mothers and children with smiles from ear to ear.

Amy Meall (11)
New Pitsligo & St Johns Primary School, Fraserburgh

Red Is . . .

A clown's big nose,
And a garden rose.

A blood pool,
And our jumpers for school.

A wobbly jelly,
And a little strawberry

A fox playing in the park,
And pretty love hearts.

My dog's cut paw,
And a lobster's sharp claw.

Kim Leith (9)
New Pitsligo & St Johns Primary School, Fraserburgh

Adolf Hitler

He's an electric chair
He's a vicious piranha
He's a ruthless raven
He's a wolf at midnight
He's a Venus flytrap
He's as dark as the night
He's a loaded gun
He's a drink of poison
He's a door always closed
He's a mad march hare!

Callum Chapman (10)
Parkhill Primary School, Leven

Saddam Hussein

He's a cooker burning rubber,
He's a chameleon always hiding and changing colour,
He's a hawk always killing his prey,
He's a dark night-time darkening the world,
He's a Venus flytrap killing his people,
He's a 'piece of cake,' so George Bush says,
He's The Joker, chasing Batman,
He's a poisoned drink killing all,
He's Saddam Hussein.

Thomas Brunton (10)
Parkhill Primary School, Leven

Robbie Williams

He's a radio chair
He's a wild monkey,
He's a colourful toucan,
He's afternoon daylight
Always singing,
He's a bright sunflower,
He's hot and spicy curry,
He's a fizzy drink,
Robbie Williams.

Chloe Kerr (11)
Parkhill Primary School, Leven

Frith's Ways

Frith has many different ways,
He made the cold, wet, winter days
He created the shining sun,
All things in the world by Lord Frith they were done,
He made our thousand enemies,
Hunters of the ground, sky, trees,
He made the yellows, reds and oranges in a sunset,
The blues in a clear sky and there's many things he'll make yet,
He made the clouds different shades of grey,
Yes, these all are from Lord Frith's ways.

Bethanie Knell (11)
Parkhill Primary School, Leven

Up At The Very Top

You can see my tree, she can as well.
So can my sister playing football.
My tree is at the very bottom of my
garden, behind my shed.
There are no birds in my tree,
or nests to get in my way.
Also there are holes in branches
that I use as rooms.
You can even climb to the top and get
a brilliant view of the country.
But the best thing is, no one else can climb it.

Sam Harvey (10)
Parkhill Primary School, Leven

Broomlee Was Great!

B ull's eye on the archery,
R opes course was great,
O n the pole climb we went,
O n the tree climb too,
M ohawk walk was good,
L ast, but not least the Flying Fox,
E gg challenge was decent,
E ggs broke and lived (our one broke!)
    Broomlee was *great!*

Callum Marley (11)
Pittenweem Primary School, Pittenweem

Football . . .

F ootball is a good sport.
O ver the years lots of teams have won.
O lympics happen every four years.
T welve teams are in the SPL.
B all games are a sport too.
A ll sports are good for you.
L iverpool is a good football team.
L eagues have a cup each year.

Ricky Bowman (11)
Pittenweem Primary School, Pittenweem

Broomlee

Broomlee is fun,
It's a good place to run,
There's plenty to do
And meet new friends too,
I liked the Flying Fox,
Better than crate climbing on a box
But now home for a rest!

Natalie Cameron (11)
Pittenweem Primary School, Pittenweem

Broomlee

We went to Broomlee on a Monday
And when we got there we said, 'Yippee!'
When we got out of the bus, we had a great fuss,
About how it would be at Broomlee.

We had horrible food!
But the puddings were good!

The toilets were stinking!
And the showers were freezing!

All the activities,
Flying Fox, problem solving, Mohawk walk, Highland games,
Music, drama and the village study,
They were all really good.

I would definitely go back to Broomlee,
Because I had so much fun.

Caitlin Wood (11)
Pittenweem Primary School, Pittenweem

Broomlee

Broomlee was good fun,
Especially the pole climb.

The dorm was comfy,
And I kept it tidy.

The games were excellent
And the food was delicious -

Especially the hot dogs!

Craig Keith (11)
Pittenweem Primary School, Pittenweem

Broomlee

Broomlee is a camp near West Linton
Where you can have fun all day,
If you go anywhere like Broomlee,
There's loads of fun coming your way!

Broomlee is a camp near West Linton
With the Flying Fox and the crate climb.
The pole climb was good, when you're in a good mood,
That's why I'm writing this rhyme!

Broomlee is a camp near West Linton
Where you can have fun all day,
If you go anywhere like Broomlee,
There's loads of fun coming your way!

Broomlee is a camp near West Linton.
Where the food is not very nice,
The dorms are the names of six different trees,
The disco at the end was *great!*

Laura Herd (11)
Pittenweem Primary School, Pittenweem

Broomlee

B ed was soft not lumpy,
R oom was clean, but dusty.
O n the rope climb it was scary,
O nly I went to the sick kids in Edinburgh!
M y arm was in a sling.
L ots of laughing and having fun.
E ating hot dogs on the last day.
E vening disco was the best!

Melissa Campbell (11)
Pittenweem Primary School, Pittenweem

Broomlee

Broomlee was good except for the food.

Rats in the toilet, that really spoiled it.

The showers were cold and covered in mould,
But still they didn't look very old.

Art and music was a lot of fun, I even played
The big bass drum.

Problem solving was the best,
It was not boring like the rest.

But most of all I like making new friends,
And that's all that matters in the end.

Jennifer Ellis (11)
Pittenweem Primary School, Pittenweem

School Trip

S houting on our journey there,
C hatting about Broomlee,
H oping it would be the best
O ut of all the rest.
O rienteering, Flying Fox,
L ooking around the village.

T ree climbing, Highland games
R unning around like idiots.
I n our dorms overnight,
P ole climb was the best!

Lianne Brunton (11)
Pittenweem Primary School, Pittenweem

Exams And Tests

Exams and tests belong in the bin,
Exams and tests, oh what a sin.
Someone must have been insane,
To invent the tests that cause us pain.

For test results we have to wait,
Exams and tests is what I hate
We wait with dread in case we fail
Don't want results to come in parent's mail.

I'll search the mail everyday,
Instead of going out to play,
If tests and exams were any worse,
I would think they were a curse.

Lois Wappler (10)
Portsoy Primary School, Portsoy

The Story Collector
(Inspired by 'The Sound Collector' by Roger McGough)

The story collector came today
He took all of our stories away
And put them in his leather sack
Then he cried, 'I'll bring them back.'

He took the short stories first
And then he took some of the worst
'All of these are really good
I'll take every story in the neighbourhood.'

Paul Lange (10)
Portsoy Primary School, Portsoy

The Tin Collector

(Inspired by 'The Sound Collector' by Roger McGough)

The tin collector came today
He took all our empty tins away
He put them in his enormous sack
And then he cried, 'I'll be back.'

'I'm just like the terminator
But this time I'm even greater,
I'll be back to collect your tins
So don't you put them in the bins.'

Ben Smith (11)
Portsoy Primary School, Portsoy

Jumping Jack

A distance jumper
A hairy hopper
A food gripper
A joey carrier
A jumping jack
A bouncing skippy
An Australian adventurer
A toothy buck.

Allan Low (11)
Rattray Primary School, Rattray

Bats

A dark hider
A silent flyer
A velvet curtain
A blurry fighter
A black fear
A screeching squeaker
A moonlight beast.

Brooke Strang (11) & Katie McIntosh
Rattray Primary School, Rattray

Shark

A meat eater
A sea swimmer
A sharp toothed beast
A fish killer
A water glider
A sea owner
A cheesy grin
A limb ripper
A sea dyer.

Steven Hooper (11)
Rattray Primary School, Rattray

Kitten

A furry ball
Smoothly purring
A little licker
A high climber
A sore scratcher
A swell eater
It is a cute feature.

Michelle Beattie (12)
Rattray Primary School, Rattray

Fish

A smooth glider
Golden skin
Big bright eyes
A floating submarine
A short memory
Lives in blue
Lives in a bowl.

Mark Stewart (11)
Rattray Primary School, Rattray

The Monkey

A cheeky chap
A banana eater
An excellent entertainer
A long leaper
A skinny screamer
A mischief maker
A branch swinger
A leaf nibbler.

Paul Maloney (11)
Rattray Primary School, Rattray

Midnight Moon

Can you see the moonlight shining very bright?
If you look at it closely it's like a shining light,
If you look at it deeply, you will eventually see,
The moon staring back at thee!

Kassie Taylor (11)
Rhynie Primary School, Huntly

From Dark To Light

She comes with birds and flowers.
She brings life back into gardens,
And makes dark places light again.
She even makes time go forward.
Maybe she'll lighten up the world,
And bring happiness to everybody again.

Peter Beeson (10)
Rhynie Primary School, Huntly

The Moonbeams

When Katie went to bed,
The moon shone on her ted,
It shone on her duvet,
The moonbeams came out to play,
She laughed and giggled,
As the moonbeams wriggled
Then they started to shiver,
Then they began to quiver,
Katie panicked,
The moonbeams went manic,
They had to go away,
But they'll be back another day!

Georgina Beeson (12)
Rhynie Primary School, Huntly

Munch, Munch, Munch

The hole punch
Has a great
Big mouth
Which goes
Munch, munch, munch.
His favourite
Food is
Beautiful paper
He hears folk
Talk and caper
About 'Lord of the Rings'
And all different things.

Lindsay Daly (12)
Rhynie Primary School, Huntly

Springtime

My gifts of clothes warm the trees,
Not like winter or autumn,
Yes, I mean leaves,
Winter is the meanest,
I am the greenest
I give lambs life
And winter strife,
Plants start growing,
It stops snowing,
My sunny face,
Looks upon the earth,
With grace,
I make my good friends, inhabitants cheerful,
And give colder seasons an earful
Of abuse,
As there is no excuse,
For making my friend, the Earth,
Lose all his mirth,
That he gained with summer's heat
And then came a sheet,
Of snow and dying,
The earth was crying,
Then I came along,
Of happiness and sun,
Ready for fun,
Sometimes out of hibernation I am late,
Though my powers are still great,
Pouring sun on ground and slate,
Of rooftops high,
Pushing ever upwards, towards the sky,
Then summer comes,
Neither early or late,
And it's time for me to hibernate,
Now I suppose I'll say goodbye,
I leave, with a sigh,
But don't worry, I haven't got the sack,
Next year, I'll be back.

Andrew Wilson (11)
Rhynie Primary School, Huntly

Sun And Rain

Why is the sun yellow?
Because it is a ball of fire.
Why is the rain wet?
Because it is drops of water.
When does it rain?
When the Earth cries.
Why does the Earth cry?
Because some humans hurt it.
Why do humans hurt it?
Because they have no respect.

Amethyst Murray (10)
Rhynie Primary School, Huntly

Springtime

I'm springtime
I watch the lambs bouncing in the field,
I see the tiny buds appearing on the trees
And I see the birds building their nests,
The grass getting greener, the flowers growing
And blossom appearing on the trees.
The temperature is getting warmer and there is longer daylight,
And it is all *thanks to me.*

Callum McIntosh (11)
Rhynie Primary School, Huntly

Cars

Cars, cars they are fast
Look after your car and it will last
Cars, cars they are alive
They are also exciting to drive.
Cars, cars they are cool
If you don't like them, then you are a fool.

Mortimer Hodge (10)
Rosehall Primary School, Lairg

A Witch's Spell

Half a pound of mouldy cake
The eyeball of a beast
The forked tongue of a snake
Some spiders for the feast.

Treacle and spice
Spoonful of mud
Salt and some mice
Worms and some blood.

One ear of a hog
Toads that are whole
A leg of a frog
All thrown in a bowl.

They all go in and are mixed about
The witch she has a grin
The one for whom this spell is made
Will soon be in a spin.

Rachael Tankard (11)
Rosehall Primary School, Lairg

Puppies

Puppies are small and very cute
And often very fluffy
They will always chew at your boots
And leave them looking scruffy

They eat your books and all your toys
And love to make a mess
Their yapping is a constant noise
Oh no! He's got Mum's dress!

He's mischievous and greedy
But also very playful
Often very needy
Never really peaceful.

Sophie Marie Baillie (10)
Rosehall Primary School, Lairg

Seasons

In summer people go on holiday
Where they swim all day
From up above the sky so high
You can see the people shopping
They look like dolls from up above

In autumn the leaves trickle
To the ground with the smallest bump
I think it's peaceful in the light breeze
I'm sure everyone does.

In winter the sky makes a blanket
Of snow on the hard ground
Going sliding down a bank
Rolling in the snow
Every snowflake has a different pattern
Like doilies at Christmas dinner.

In spring the days get longer
The lambs scurry around
Playing with one another
The stars in the night sky
Twinkle like stardust in the
Hanging moonlight.

Anneke Ekema (11)
Rosehall Primary School, Lairg

Dogs

Dogs are loving
Dogs are caring
They will play with you
Anytime.
They love you
You love them
That's the special thing
About you and them.

Jordan Morrison (11)
Rosehall Primary School, Lairg

A Magic Potion

One wing of a fly
And some lightening from the sky
A few drops of green gloopy goo
Mix it up and stir it around
Then add two drops of blood
Three warts from a toad
And five hairs from a smelly dog
Then the next person I see will turn into a toad.

Hannah Stevens (9)
Rosehall Primary School, Lairg

My Pet Rabbit

If I had a rabbit, it would be golden,
Her name would be Goldy.
Every day I would play with her,
She would be soft so I could hug her,
I would sit her on my knee,
She would get five carrots a day.

Liah Stevens (8)
Rosehall Primary School, Lairg

Maths

M ental maths is good for your brain
A dding and subtracting, I love them both.
T imesing and dividing is always hard
H arder and harder dividing gets
S o I often need a day off.

Liam Spence (8)
Rosehall Primary School, Lairg

A Big Eye

A big eye
A simple cry.

A pink pad
They'll go mad.

A wet nose
And small toes.

A floppy ear
A loyal peer.

A long tongue
A smelly dung.

A cute face
A slow pace.

A waggy tail
A sharp wail.

A nosy mind
All sweet and kind.

A funny K9
He is all mine

A catalogue to make me puppy.

Jacklyn McConachie (11)
St Blanes Primary School, Glasgow

The Wind

A cold drizzle
A scary whistle
A wet blow
A freaky glow
A hard wind
A new top binned
A catalogue to make me wind.

Magen Donnelly (12)
St Blanes Primary School, Glasgow

The Two Day Kill

The cock did crow one winter's day,
The land was white with snow,
Sweet Mary woke up from her sleep,
Fearing not friend nor foe.
She smiled out to all the town,
And waved up to the sky,
Alas, poor girl, she didn't know
That danger lurked near by.
She went next door to say hello
To her dear good-hearted neighbour,
Expecting not an evil man
Just to come and slay her.
She was grabbed and took away,
Her cries were muffled out
By her 'nappers hairy hands,
Oh so short and stout.

The cock did crow the morning after
She was nowhere to be found,
If only her family knew,
He'd taken her underground.
There he'd tied her to a pole
And hit her on the head
And Mary knew that soon that day
She would probably be dead.
He was a man who should be caught
And put in jail for life.
But as she thought her own last thoughts,
The man pulled out a knife.
'We'll remember Mary, now and forever,
Her memory will never sever.'

Nicole Barrett (11)
St Blanes Primary School, Glasgow

Seasons

All the flowers growing fast
It's funny how the grass is always last,
The sun comes out and starts shining,
And all the kids stop whining.

Summer comes bright and nice
Makes the kids bring out the ice
Water fights all the time
Making fun every time.

Autumn comes with a blow
All the kids go with the flow,
All the leaves falling down,
Makes the kids go round and round.

Autumn goes fast and quick
Winter comes without a tick,
All the snow nice and white
You can always have a snowball fight.

Paul Stuart (11)
St Blanes Primary School, Glasgow

Night's Change

It was a dark and horror night
And through Graham's window was a scary sight.
The stars and moon were shining
Then the shining stopped and the thunder came blasting.

When the night had turned to day
Graham had went outside to play
When Graham had come inside
He wanted to go out again, but it was too dark outside.

That night it was a calm and peaceful night
And through Graham's window was a lovely sight.
The stars and moon were shining,
But this time it did stay shining.

Gordon Bushby (11)
St Blanes Primary School, Glasgow

Different Months Of The Year

January is a nice month, but it is too cold.
Just after Christmas I play with everything just like gold.
February has only twenty-eight days
I sometimes have long lies.

March and it's near my birthday
I'd love to have a dirt bike on my birthday
April and it is near Easter Sunday
And it was very sunny.

May and some Primary 4s are taking their communion,
Some of them are going to have a reunion,
June and we are going on our school trip soon,
I liked the song on the bus, it was a catchy tune.

July and we are going to France,
I met a man called Lance,
August and I went to the swimming pool,
I am starting secondary school.

Martin Wright (12)
St Blanes Primary School, Glasgow

Space

Space is where the aliens rule
Space is where they go to school
Space is where they eat their food
Space is where they go in a mood.

Space is where the planets are
From earth they are very, very far
Space is where Pluto's small
Space is where Jupiter's tall.

Space is where stars are at
Some small and some are fat
They go into clusters at the Milky Way
Then they break, that's the way.

Connor Downie (11)
St Blanes Primary School, Glasgow

Fun Classroom

Welcome to our classroom
Where everything is fun
No one is ever filled with glum
Even if our work is not done
We have the school's biggest classroom
Which is great to hold our treasure. . . *fun*

Let's introduce to you Group One the laughable lions
Laughable by name and by nature
You will never see them crying
Laughing they will capture
All the time until they're dying
They may get into trouble therefore

Now let's hear from the Hyper Hippos
One says we love our teacher
Although she is really hippy
At PE she is a real peacher
Her long hair reminds them of Pippy
And the hippy teacher is what puts hyper in Hyper Hippos.

Nicole Fallon (12)
St Blanes Primary School, Glasgow

Guess Who?

A hard worker
A forgetful stepper
Back bender
A sore toe
A tired girl
A good posture
A tight bunner
A sore header
A smelly sweater
A costume changer
An even better legger
A first place collector
An all day dancer!

Joanne Walker (11)
St Blanes Primary School, Glasgow

Chocolate

When I opened that cupboard
And oh yes!
Just guess
Oh eating a bar of chocolate

As I slowly tear open that chocolate bar
My mouth watered and dribbles
I just want to taste some tasty nibbles
Oh eating a bar of chocolate

Slowly and steadily, I aim for my mouth
I fire, I score
Mmm, my mouth snores
Oh eating a bar of chocolate

Chocolate is good to eat
It's gooey and creamy
And all so dreamy
Oh, eating a bar of chocolate.

Holly J McDougall (11)
St Blanes Primary School, Glasgow

If I Won The Lottery

If I won the lottery
This is what I'd get
A big house, a fancy car
But you've heard nothing yet

 A room made of chocolate
A swimming pool too
My very own ice rink
And a super big zoo

But the thing that I would have to get
Would definitely be
An enormous shopping mall
And all of it for me.

Sophie McCullagh (11)
St Blanes Primary School, Glasgow

My Best Friend

My best friend is always neat . . .
From the top of her head,
To the bottom of her feet.
She really likes to dance and sing
Pop and dance music are her favourite thing.
She swims like a dolphin in the sea.

She is really funny
Sometimes reminds me of a bunny,
Really sweet, always smiles
Always there, hair nice and fair.
Ears like an owl's to listen with care.
Dancing around filled with glee
Make-up, shoes and clothes make her happy.
Smart and bright, filled with delight
Always getting stuff right.

Her room is always nice and tidy
Pink and sweet, big and that
Making noises while she sleeps
'Like a snoring noise, but much worse.'
I must be lucky to have a friend like that!

Shaughn Meechan (11)
St Blanes Primary School, Glasgow

Apples

Apples, apples sure so yummy
Apples, apples good for my tummy
Apples, apples are so sweet
Apples, apples they are a good treat

Apples, apples good for eating
Apples, apples everyone meeting
Apples, apples are so yummy
Apples, apples for my tummy.

Lisa McAdams (11)
St Blanes Primary School, Glasgow

My Mouse Is Different

My little mouse's name is Harry,
When you lift him, he's easy to carry,
He's black and white and lovely and furry,
And the thing he loves most is his chicken curry,
He's got tiny feet and a pointed nose,
But he hates getting soaked by the hose,
He loves nibbling on cheese and things,
He even likes to nibble on my rings,
He's really cute and really quiet,
But when he eats he causes a riot.
He loves children and likes to play
Even on a rainy day.
There is a cat in the house,
But he doesn't mind my little mouse.
I know he's unhappy when he sits,
So I cheer him up, because I love him to bits.

Alix Hutcheson (11)
St Blanes Primary School, Glasgow

Stars

A bright light
A starry night
Dancing surprises
Wow! What a sight
Silently twinkling
Happy and shining
Shooting and falling
Ever so bright
Stars are best friends
In a friendship that never ends
In a constellation
They shine over the nation.

Natalie Lester (12)
St Blanes Primary School, Glasgow

The Beach

What about the scorching sun?
I think it is very fun.
People burning all around
Then someone with a tan is finally found
The sunburn gives you a lot of pain,
At least you're not in the rain.

What about the saltwater sea?
The smell really puts off me,
But, it's good on the pedalo,
Because you don't have to row, row, row.
The jet-skis are very fast
The little shrimps are washed away at last.

What about the golden sand?
I wish it was all over the land
'Why is the sand so hot?' they say,
Because the sun beats on it all day.
There are buckets and spades
Big sandcastles are made.

What about the children who play?
All day they will stay
How do they not pass out
When they always jump about
Burying their dads in the sand
Instead of clapping their hands.

Liam McLaughlin (11)
St Blanes Primary School, Glasgow

The Sandwich

My, oh, my I need something to eat,
Sandwich, a sandwich! That'll be my treat.
So I go to the fridge and search up and down,
Cheese, lettuce and bread that is brown.
I search harder and harder and find some more toppings
Now I'm excited, I'm like Mary Poppins.

I start to spread with lots of my butter,
Concentrating hard, I didn't even mutter.
Time for tomatoes, lettuce and cheese,
My sandwich says, 'Salt and pepper please.'
A little drop of onions and a slice of cold meat,
My cold cut combo . . . a precious treat.

I'll sit my sandwich on a plate
Cut it in half, get ready to be ate,
I lick my lips like a big grizzly bear,
My sandwich wishes it was hiding somewhere.
I really can't wait to the very first bite,
Because half the sandwich will be out of sight.

So off I go to take a bite,
The melting sandwich is such a delight
I munch all the rest in a flash
I could make another and sell it for cash,
Now I've had my sandwich, I'm going for a rest,
With no doubt, my sandwich was the best.

Dean Burnett (11)
St Blanes Primary School, Glasgow

Easter Rabbit

I saw a little bunny go
Hop, hop, hop.
So I said, 'Little bunny please
Stop, stop, stop.'
The bunny was eating some chocolate
Eggs, eggs, eggs
As he was hopping on his two back
Legs, legs, legs.
I wanted some chocolate eggs to
Eat, eat, eat
So I will have to race the little bunny,
But also cheat, cheat, cheat.
That little bunny is very
Fast, fast, fast
But I'll try not to come in
Last, last, last.
The bunny hopped over to me on his
Two back legs, legs, legs
And asked me if I would like some chocolate
Eggs, eggs, eggs
I said, 'OK,' in shock, shock, shock
Then I went away with a very happy
Walk, walk, walk!

Kyle Wands (12)
St Blanes Primary School, Glasgow

Sweets, Sweets, Sweets!

Galaxy, Milky Way and Magic Stars
Sweets and the solar system don't match by far
Chunky Double Deckers and fruit filled Picnics
Just the names make me want to lick my lips
Now the nation's favourite, the ones we all know
Dairy Milk, Mars and Maltesers
The ones that help us grow

Sugar rush from bubblegum makes you want to hop
Take it out the packet, chew it, blow and pop!
Fini booms and grey eyeballs, cavities galore
Endless appointments at the dentist, more and more and more

Crunchy, munchy, chomping, gnawing, parking round my mouth
Dripping, licking, sticking, picking, children never pout
Mint chips, honeycomb and mini-marshmallows too
All these sounds tantalise your tongue, oh yes I can see you!
Surprising Revels what's in each one?
Chocolate, toffee, coffee and more
Scraping it off my thumb.

Jennifer Ann Calder (11)
St Blanes Primary School, Glasgow

Happiness

Happiness is a bright orange
It tastes like a ripe strawberry
It smells like fresh baking
Happiness looks like a ray of sunshine
It sounds like birds singing in the morning
And feels good.

Eilidh McCadden (11)
St Francis Of Assisi Primary School, Cumbernauld

Theseus And The Minotaur

The Minotaur was a fierce beast
He liked to eat people for a feast
The people that came in the labyrinth didn't live long
After he killed them he sang a little song
He would sing,
'I can kill anybody I want,
I can,
I can,
I can'
He thought this until Theseus came along
He was only halfway through the song
Theseus fought and tried to be brave
To send the Minotaur to his grave
Now in the 21st Century the Minotaur's gone
But was it all a *big huge* con?
Read some books and you might find
That the Minotaur wasn't so kind!

Roisin Miller (11)
St Francis Of Assisi Primary School, Cumbernauld

My Little Hamster

My little hamster, Sparkle's her name
My little hamster she glows like a flame
She's like a teddy so small so sweet
And if she's good I give her treat
My little hamster's white and light brown
My little hamster never has a frown
She loves her exercise she's so fast
And she wishes her exercise would always last
My little hamster loves being out of her cage
If she isn't she shows me her rage
My little hamster's so much fun
She's cool she sparkles she's my number one.

Michael Hamilton (10)
St Francis Of Assisi Primary School, Cumbernauld

The Headless Horseman Of Sleepy Hollow

One night, a woman got a terrible fright
She was washing the floor with a mop
Suddenly, clip clop, clip clop
The woman ran in fear
Because she knew the headless horsemen was here.

Sleepy Hollow is a terrible place
The town is really going to waste
For every night a head is found.

The bridge is where the headless horseman lives
So never go near
On the stroke of midnight he gallops by
No one really knows why.

Hallowe'en is his favourite night
Despite the fact
That no one comes out.

So whenever the moon is set
Whenever the wind is high
The Headless Horseman
Goes riding by.

Andrew Doherty (11)
St Francis Of Assisi Primary School, Cumbernauld

The Great Galloper

Watch as he gallops down the street
Listen as his horse makes a steady beat
Faster and faster he goes
Quickly riding by the crows
Watch in horror as he strikes the innocent
And leaves them on the road
Who is he? You wonder
Riding to the noise of thunder
He is the Great Galloper.

Daniel Rudden (10)
St Francis Of Assisi Primary School, Cumbernauld

The Beggar

There is a beggar at the end of my street
No one knows but his name is Pete
Every time I pass him by I hold my nose
I once suggested he should wash his clothes

Pete used to be married with two children
Named Matt and Pat
They still live in the family home with Henry their fat cat
A far place from Pete who is out in the wet
But yet he does not forget

Pete, Pete, Pete

People just walk by
And I the little girl with the yellow top wonder why.

Roisin Donnelly (9)
St Francis Of Assisi Primary School, Cumbernauld

In The Night

In the night
I feel fright
I have a fear
That ghosts are near.

I don't want to say
Just hope they go
Away if I close
My eyes tight
It will be alright.

In the morning
They've all gone
And I am glad
That it is dawn.

Jacob McCann (9)
St Francis Of Assisi Primary School, Cumbernauld

Travel With Me

Tickets are booked
Flights are paid
I hope we have a friendly maid.

A day in the car
A sail on a ship
How I love to plan our trips.

The thrill of take off on a plane
Really tickles my tummy
But it's a pity the food's not
Yummy!

I love to travel, it's such fun,
And all of my family like
To relax in the sun!

I've been to many different countries
I couldn't name them all
I've been to some when I was tall
And even when I was small

I started in my early years
I was only 12 weeks old.

My first port of call was Majorca
And then my travels unfold.

Asia, Europe wherever we are
We always like to travel afar.

The world is my oyster.

Alexandra Lawson (9)
St Francis Of Assisi Primary School, Cumbernauld

Seaside

At the seaside the waves crash
And you don't need to spend lots of cash
You sit and relax
No need to worry because no one is in a hurry
You can make sandcastles and splash in the sea
And have fun all day
You can sit in the sun and eat ice cream all day
And dream all your cares away.

Lisa Divers (10)
St Francis Of Assisi Primary School, Cumbernauld

The Colour Yellow

The yellow colour is everywhere, look at these:
I can see the big golden sun.
I can hear the yellow beautiful butterflies
Flapping their wings.
I can smell wet dripping dried grass
I can touch slippery yellow banana skin
And all of these make me feel warm
Dozy and snugly.

Rüyana Rüzgar (9)
St Leonards Primary School, Dunfermline

The Colour Yellow

The lovely hot sand on the beach
Autumn yellow leaves in the breeze
Mum's making fresh bread, mmm.
I can touch rusty yellow leaves falling
I now feel excited for my warm bread.

Lauren Gallagher (9)
St Leonards Primary School, Dunfermline

Blue

I can see gannets swooping into
The glittering sea to catch some fish.

I can smell the blue whale splashing
Glittery water back into the sea.

I can hear the small bluetits in a
Light and soft nesting box waiting for their mother.

I can touch the blue blossoms on the tree
Where the light and homely nest box is.

I feel calm, slowly by lying on
The shore.

Lisa Malpas (9)
St Leonards Primary School, Dunfermline

The Colour Blue

The beautiful waterfall whooshing down the rocks
The shiny flat water swaying in the sea.
Juicy blueberries falling off the trees.
The hard blue map in the classroom
It makes me feel like I want to go swimming.

Jack Adamson (8)
St Leonards Primary School, Dunfermline

Blue

I can see the sparkling bright sea
I can hear the water bashing against rocks
I can smell blue food colouring on a delicious cake
I can touch the surfboards and crashing waves
I can feel soaking wet from the sea.

Samuel O'Brien (8)
St Leonards Primary School, Dunfermline

Red Is The Best

I can see the red warm fire
Going up and down and hands going near
It and people saying, 'Ooh, ahh.'
Mum shouting at the top of her voice
Screaming at the end of the stairs.
I can touch red yummy plums rolling
From the trees all day
Red coconut icing that is lovely
And just want to eat it.
Burning hot head on me
When I'm hot.

Hayley Gibson (8)
St Leonards Primary School, Dunfermline

The Colour Blue

I can see my own country's flag
I can hear waves splashing in the sea.
I can smell a gentle calm breeze.
I can touch a glowing brightness of the colour blue.
Then I feel thrilled and full of joy.

Sean MacGregor (9)
St Leonards Primary School, Dunfermline

Blue

I can see Dunfermline playing football really well
I can smell the tough, mad, breezy wind.
I can hear strong sea splashing people.
I can touch blue shirts with long sleeves
I feel like dozing off on a fluffy blue pillow.

Louis Wain (8)
St Leonards Primary School, Dunfermline

Blue

I can see the colour blue
It's the colour of very deep water.
A splashing sound in the sea.
I can touch the very big waterfall
Blueberry pie ready to be cooked
I can feel very energetic.

Cameron Campbell (8)
St Leonards Primary School, Dunfermline

The Colour Yellow

I can see the sandy castles at the beach
I can hear the daffodils growing up, up
And through the soil.
I can smell the sticky sun in the sky.
I can touch a yellow leaf.
I can feel lovely cats' fur.

Ashley Kendall (8)
St Leonards Primary School, Dunfermline

Yellow

The lovely sunflowers in the garden
The sand moving by the wind on the beach
The yellow custard cooked by my mum
The yellow corn in the field getting ripened
I feel excited because of the hot sun
Shining on my face.

Joeanne Nicol (9)
St Leonards Primary School, Dunfermline

Passionate Blue

I can see the ocean stretched out like a strong soft blanket.
I can touch clear unpolluted water in an untouched sparkling river.
I can hear the great rush of the wind.
I can smell crisp air whipping my hair back.
I can feel ready and willing for any task.

Emily Christie (8)
St Leonards Primary School, Dunfermline

The Colour Yellow

I can see the beautiful yellow sun shining down from the blue sky.
I can smell the yellow sun baking on your skin.
I can hear the yellow flapping flowers waving at me.
I can touch the yellow soft pale flowers and
I can feel the happy expression coming up on my face.

Claire Aitchison (8)
St Leonards Primary School, Dunfermline

Yellow

The yellow sand waving.
The yellow leaves blowing away.
The yellow star fruits.
The yellow pillows.
I feel excited with joy.

John Lessels (10)
St Leonards Primary School, Dunfermline

Orange

I can see the burning sun in the morning.
I can hear the loudness of a lion roaring.
I can smell the meaty breath of a tiger as he roars.
I can touch the boiling tomato soup on a cold night.
I can feel cuddly and comfy sleeping in my bed.

Andrew Sherriffs (8)
St Leonards Primary School, Dunfermline

Glowing Orange

Colourful orange leaves blowing in the wind.
Sprouting orange tulips in the summer.
Sparkling bright, strong orange diamonds
My sister's hair in an orange ribbon
So summery.

Heather Dunn (8)
St Leonards Primary School, Dunfermline

Blue

The sparkling cold waves
A cold trickling river
Rotten smelly fish
My cold blue sharpener
Water dripping off me.

Mark Keir (9)
St Leonards Primary School, Dunfermline

Red

The red shining scooter in the hot sun.
A puddle of red wine dripping, drip-drop.
A burning fire in the night.
The red plum in my hand, yum, yum.
My red heart pounding.

Liam Morton (8)
St Leonards Primary School, Dunfermline

The Colour Yellow

I can see the sun shining down on me.
I can hear people spreading butter on toast.
I can smell the daffodils through the air.
I can feel the sun shining in the air.
I can feel the brightness burning my skin.

Brandon Bryce (8)
St Leonards Primary School, Dunfermline

Green

Lovely squirrels in the green grass playing.
The lovely trees swaying and going side to side.
Lovely fresh apples just been made.
Soft green pillows, it makes you
Feel tired, calm and cooled down.

Chelsea Trotter (8)
St Leonards Primary School, Dunfermline

My Feelings For Orange

I can see the beautiful sunset orange in the sky.
I can hear the juice squirting from the carton.
I can smell the lovely smelling orange coconut ice.
I can touch rough oranges in my hand.
I can feel very happy and energetic.

Michael Kerr (8)
St Leonards Primary School, Dunfermline

A Sports Poem

Football is excellent
Footballers wear lots of different colours
Footballers play in lots of different countries
Footballers play with lots of different balls

Swimmers are good at swimming
Swimming pools are everywhere
Swimmers are good at swimming
Swimmers swim in different countries

Running is good for you
Runners are good at jumping over stuff
Everyone can run until they are old
Runners can have fun running

Wrestlers are really strong
Wrestlers have matches all the time
Wrestlers are bad to people
Wrestlers always want to win.

Kieron Treanor (8)
Sea View School, Kirkcaldy

Dog

A dog is fast at running
A dog is fun to play with
Brown, black, white and grey
All different colours

A dog can run very fast
A dog can eat lots of food
It's collar is red and blue
It's lead is green and pink

A dog likes food, especially biscuits
A dog likes walks to the beach
After a walk it needs a drink
Or maybe a treat that is yummy

A dog can bark very loud
A dog can see in black and white
If you stay with him
You will see just how clever he can be.

Emily Doherty (7)
Sea View School, Kirkcaldy

The Seasons

Spring is the season where flowers grow
The time when rivers flow
I like very much the season of spring
Thank you God for everything

Summer is when the fun begins
And the time when birds sing
This is the time to become lazy
The sky now becomes hazy

Autumn is the time when leaves fall
The time when you play with a ball
It is the time when wind blows
Next comes the season of snow

Winter is the time for joy
It is also the time for girls and boys
It is the season when Santa Claus comes
Every one is having fun.

Holly Jones (8)
Sea View School, Kirkcaldy

A Friend

A friend is cheerful and nice
A friend does not scream and a friend is everything
A friend plays with you when you're lonely
A friend is good because he's happy

A friend is there for you when you're unhappy
A friend is a mate
A friend likes to do things
A friend is smart and bright

A friend does good things for you
A friend is good for you
A friend likes you
A friend is very funny

My friend is very silly
My friend likes football like me
My friend is good at maths and I'm sure he's good at language
My friend likes rounders and football.

Nicholas Diston (8)
Sea View School, Kirkcaldy

Seasons

In spring the baby lambs are born
Shorts and T-shirts can be worn
Sitting in a tent eating nice food
Going for a walk in the lovely woods

In summer it is hot
Play outside with the chalk
Wear sandals at the beach
To get your sunglasses you have to reach

In the autumn it is a bit cool
Now we have to go back to school
The breeze is fast and very quick
You can throw a stick

In winter it starts to snow
You can make a snowman you know
With a hat, scarf, two stone eyes and a carrot nose
Who comes in this season? Everyone knows!

Hannah Wood (7)
Sea View School, Kirkcaldy

Pirates

Pirates are ugly and gruesome
They kill everyone to get money
Jack Sparrow is my favourite one
He is very weird and strong

Pirates' buried treasure on an island
They are extremely rich and usually drunk
Their ships are fantastically tall
There ships are also long

Pirates have pet parrots and dogs
Their parrots are so noisy
Their dogs bark very noisily too
They loved to sing happy songs

Pirates are horrible but good sailors
My favourite ship is the Queen Ann's Revenge
Pirates are interesting for me
You'll have to walk the plank if you do something wrong.

William Dineen (8)
Sea View School, Kirkcaldy

Games In The Playground

Hide-and-seek, don't peek
Running to a hiding place
Race the others to that hiding place
You can hide high, you can hide low
But whatever you do, don't go slow

Skipping 1, 2, 3
I'm in Primary 3
Come on skip with me
These are hard.
You are good at skipping too

Catch me, catch me
If you can
Two more seconds until I run
Now you're here with me
Come on tig me

Some play rough
Some play tough
Some are sad
Some are bad
Games are fun.

Danny Dineen (7)
Sea View School, Kirkcaldy

Ugly Bugs

Bees, bees they are bright
Bees, bees they are yellow
Bees, bees they are black
Bees, bees they have six legs

Ladybirds have dots on their back
Ladybirds have six legs
Ladybirds live in your grass
Ladybirds come out in summer

Slugs are slimy
Slugs are gooey
Slugs are greeny-brown
Slugs have no legs

Worms, worms they are yuck!
Worms, worms they won't be tasty
Worms, worms they have no legs
Worms, worms they live in the earth

Butterflies are very colourful
Caterpillars turn into a butterfly
Caterpillars go into a cocoon
Butterflies can fly very high.

Laura Innes (8)
Sea View School, Kirkcaldy

Wrestling

Wrestling, wrestling, they enter with a thunder
Fireworks, bright lights go off everywhere
They come out in the ring
The crowd go really hyper

Wrestling, wrestling they come down to the ring
They beat each other up
The ref counts 1,2,3
The crowd go really hyper

Wrestling, wrestling I love it
My favourite wrestler is The Undertaker
They have lots of matches
The crowd go really hyper

Wrestling, wrestling it moves around a lot
From London to New York
It is on all day long, 10 o'clock to 1 o'clock
The crowd go really hyper.

Robbie Gavin (9)
Sea View School, Kirkcaldy

The Sloth Poem

Would you like to be like me
Hanging upside down all day long
I live on the branches of trees
And I sleep on the branches of trees
My coat can be any colour from brown to grey to white
I eat leaves, fruit and shoots all day long
My top speed is 1 mile per hour
I live in South America's rainforest.

Robert Sinclair (12)
Stoneywood Primary School, Aberdeen

I'm A Piranha

Huh, I'm a piranha
I'm a piranha
As my eyes beam
Creatures scream
I am sad
People think I'm bad
I have no family at all
I've eaten them all
I'm a plranha
I'm a piranha
I have got sharp jaws
That cut through food like chainsaws
I'm all alone
I'm all alone
I've eaten everything to bone
I wait at the bottom of the river
And wait for someone to linger
I can be many different colours
Blue, red, orange, green and white
You never know I just might
Take a bite
Would you like to be a piranha?
Would you?

Ross Soutar (11)
Stoneywood Primary School, Aberdeen

A Viking

There was a Viking from France who always pooped his pants
At the first sight of battle he would shake and he would rattle
And couldn't even defeat cattle
He turned around to get a snack
When he got a dagger in the back
Then his ghost came from the past
Then he couldn't fight the blast.

Ian Lawson (12)
Stoneywood Primary School, Aberdeen

The Race To Space

The 2066 Weetabix rocket race to space
The bird, dog and frog
The bird from Lurd
The dog from Bog
The frog from Nog
The people scared of them dying whilst they were flying
3,2,1 they set off one by one
They went at speeds off 1888 miles an hour
They saw an alien but they couldn't talk to it
They had a race to win
They finished in this order
The frog from Nog
The dog from Bog
The bird from Lurd.

Lewis Gary Taylor (12)
Stoneywood Primary School, Aberdeen

Chocolate

Chocolate is yummy
Chocolate is scrummy
It melts in your mouth
It melts in your tummy
Because it is yummy
But the kind of chocolate I like
Is the kind that is nice and creamy
I like chocolate, do you?

Brian Harley (10)
Torbain Primary School, Kirkcaldy

My Big Sister

My big sister is a pain
She annoys me constantly again and again
She gets annoyed at the least wee thing
She gets paranoid at everything
What I'm trying to say is my sister is lovely, but a pain!

Sarah Fleming (9)
Torbain Primary School, Kirkcaldy

Limerick

There was a young man from Skye
Who stuck his head in a pie
He took his head out
And looked all about
And discovered that he could never fly.

Robbie Balfour (10)
Torbain Primary School, Kirkcaldy

My Limerick

There was a young girl called Heather
Who was very fond of sunny weather
In the sun she would lie
And wish she could fly
Right up to the sky like a feather.

Heather Moore (8)
Townhill Primary School, Hamilton

A Hunter's Mind

Look at how they run as we hunt them with our guns
Look at how they hide in the wide open spaces
Just look at how they cower at our fantastic power
Just give it up seal pup!

Jessica Secmezsoy Urquhart (10)
Townhill Primary School, Hamilton

My Limerick

There once was a girl called Emma
Who had a friend called Gemma
Should they go the park?
Or have a tart?
That was their dilemma.

Emma Gordon (10)
Townhill Primary School, Hamilton

My Limerick

There once was a girl called Lyns
Who was incredibly light on her pins
She went into a trance
When she started to dance
Though her job was just emptying bins.

Lynsey Smith (10)
Townhill Primary School, Hamilton

There Once Was A Young Girl

There once was a young girl called Emma Keir
Who rowed a boat and travelled far and near
She was chased by a shark
Until it turned dark
And ended up beside Blackpool Pier!

Emma Keir (9)
Townhill Primary School, Hamilton

My Trick

There was once a girl called Nick
She could do a very good trick
She could bounce a ball into a hall
And that proved she wasn't thick.

Nicola Wilson (10)
Townhill Primary School, Hamilton

A Loodicrous Tale

There was a wee lass her name was Kirsten
She opened the class door and suddenly burst in
A story she had - she was dying to tell
The toilets were blocked and had a bad smell
The girl who had been using it was terribly thin
After flushing it she had been sucked in!

Kirsten Maclean (9)
Townhill Primary School, Hamilton

Katie's Mate

There was once a girl called Kate
Who had a very nice mate
Her name was Wendy
And she was very trendy
And she was always very late.

Katie Fairfull (9)
Townhill Primary School, Hamilton

My Limerick

There once was a young girl called Emma
And she had a dog called Gemma
Her dog fell down a hole
That went to the North Pole
And now Emma has a dilemma.

Emma Caldwell (9)
Townhill Primary School, Hamilton